G000320676

Low-fat Cookbook

HAMLYN DIETPLAN SERIES

Low-fat
Cookbook

Beth Cockburn-Smith

HAMLYN

London · New York · Sydney · Toronto

The following titles are also available in this series:

Arthritic Cookbook · Cooking for a Healthy Baby
Diabetic Cookbook · Low-sodium Cookbook

The following titles are available in the Hamlyn Cookshelf series:

Biscuits and Cookies · Chilli Cookbook ·Cooking with Yogurt
Food Processor Cookbook · Mighty Mince Cookbook
Potato Cookery · Sweets and Candies

Consultant nutritionist: Jenny Salmon
Photography by David Johnson
Line drawings by Ann Rees

First published in 1984 by
Hamlyn Publishing
a division of The Hamlyn Publishing Group Limited
Bridge House, London Road, Twickenham, Middlesex, England

Some of this material was originally published in either *Cooking for your
Heart's Sake* or *Cooking with Yogurt*

ISBN 0 600 32406 0

Set in Monophoto Photina
by Servis Filmsetting Limited, Manchester, England

Printed in Yugoslavia

Contents

Useful Facts and Figures

Notes on metrication

In this book quantities are given in metric and Imperial measures. Exact conversion from Imperial to metric measures does not usually give very convenient working quantities and so the metric measures have been rounded off into units of 25 grams. The table below shows the recommended equivalents.

Ounces	Approx. g to nearest whole figure	Recommended conversion to nearest unit of 25	Ounces	Approx. g to nearest whole figure	Recommended conversion to nearest unit of 25
1	28	25	11	312	300
2	57	50	12	340	350
3	85	75	13	368	375
4	113	100	14	396	400
5	142	150	15	425	425
6	170	175	16 (1 lb)	454	450
7	198	200	17	482	475
8	227	225	18	510	500
9	255	250	19	539	550
10	283	275	20 (1¼ lb)	567	575

Note: When converting quantities over 20 oz first add the appropriate figures in the centre column, then adjust to the nearest unit of 25. As a general guide, 1 kg (1000 g) equals 2.2 lb or about 2 lb 3 oz. This method of conversion gives good results in nearly all cases, although in certain pastry and cake recipes a more accurate conversion is necessary to produce a balanced recipe.

Liquid measures The millilitre has been used in this book and the following table gives a few examples.

Imperial	Approx. ml to nearest whole figure	Recommended ml	Imperial	Approx. ml to nearest whole figure	Recommended ml
¼ pint	142	150 ml	1 pint	567	600 ml
½ pint	283	300 ml	1½ pints	851	900 ml
¾ pint	425	450 ml	1¼ pints	992	1000 ml (1 litre)

Spoon measures All spoon measures are level unless otherwise stated.
Can sizes At present, cans are marked with the exact (usually to the nearest whole number) metric equivalent of the Imperial weight of the contents, so we have followed this practice when giving can sizes.

Oven temperatures
The table below gives recommended equivalents.

	°C	°F	Gas Mark		°C	°F	Gas Mark
Very cool	110	225	$\frac{1}{4}$	Moderately hot	190	375	5
	120	250	$\frac{1}{2}$		200	400	6
Cool	140	275	1	Hot	220	425	7
	150	300	2		230	450	8
Moderate	160	325	3	Very hot	240	475	9
	180	350	4				

Notes for American and Australian users

In America the 8-fl oz measuring cup is used. In Australia metric measures are now used in conjunction with the standard 250-ml measuring cup. The Imperial pint, used in Britain and Australia, is 20 fl oz, while the American pint is 16 fl oz. It is important to remember that the Australian tablespoon differs from both the British and American tablespoons; the table below gives a comparison. The British standard tablespoon, which has been used throughout this book, holds 17.7 ml, the American 14.2 ml, and the Australian 20 ml. A teaspoon holds approximately 5 ml in all three countries.

British	American	Australian
1 teaspoon	1 teaspoon	1 teaspoon
1 tablespoon	1 tablespoon	1 tablespoon
2 tablespoons	3 tablespoons	2 tablespoons
$3\frac{1}{2}$ tablespoons	4 tablespoons	3 tablespoons
4 tablespoons	5 tablespoons	$3\frac{1}{2}$ tablespoons

An Imperial/American guide to solid and liquid measures

Imperial	American	Imperial	American
SOLID MEASURES		LIQUID MEASURES	
1 lb butter or		$\frac{1}{4}$ pint liquid	$\frac{2}{3}$ cup liquid
margarine	2 cups	$\frac{1}{2}$ pint	$1\frac{1}{4}$ cups
1 lb flour	4 cups	$\frac{3}{4}$ pint	2 cups
1 lb granulated or		1 pint	$2\frac{1}{2}$ cups
caster sugar	2 cups	$1\frac{1}{2}$ pints	$3\frac{3}{4}$ cups
1 lb icing sugar	3 cups	2 pints	5 cups
8 oz rice	1 cup		($2\frac{1}{2}$ pints)

NOTE: When making any of the recipes in this book, only follow one set of measures as they are not interchangeable.

Introduction

Why low fat? There are two compelling reasons for making sure that meals don't contain large amounts of fat – better health and a slimmer figure. Low-fat eating is one sure way of improving overall health and it's also one of the easiest ways of losing weight – if you need to. But 'low fat' does not mean 'no fat'. Quite apart from the fact that some fat is essential for health, a fat-free diet is extremely unpleasant to eat. And you'd need to eat very large amounts of fat-free foods to get enough energy to live on and to maintain weight.

Different kinds of fats Although we talk about fat as though it were a single compound, there are, in fact, many different kinds of fats, which have different functions.

The fats in foods are properly called triglycerides. Each fat consists of a glycerol backbone with three fatty acids attached to it. Each fatty acid is a chain – of variable length – made mainly of carbon and hydrogen. Each carbon atom can 'hold', at most, two hydrogen atoms. If all the carbon atoms have their two hydrogens, the fatty acid is called a saturated fatty acid. And if most of the fatty acids in the food are saturated, we talk about a saturated fat. Examples are butter, cream, cheese and meat fat.

If, however, two of the carbon atoms are short of hydrogen, that fatty acid is called a mono-unsaturated fatty acid. An example is olive oil.

If four or more of the carbon atoms are short of hydrogen, the fatty acid is a polyunsaturated one.

When the proportion of polyunsaturated fatty acids in the whole fat is high, we talk about polyunsaturated fats. Examples are certain kinds of margarine, sunflower seed oil, corn oil and some other vegetable and fish oils.

When margarine is made from liquid vegetable oils, hydrogen is added to the fatty acids so that they become more saturated and, at the same time, harder. So it is quite likely that a polyunsaturated vegetable oil becomes a saturated margarine. But, by using special techniques, it is possible to mix together a very hard (saturated) fat and a very soft (polyunsaturated) fat so that the final margarine is high in polyunsaturates, and is at the same time soft enough to spread from the fridge but hard enough to be manageable.

How much fat do we need? At the moment the average amount of fat eaten in a typical Western diet is about 128 g a day for every person. This includes the obvious fatty foods like butter, meat fat, cream and salad oil, but also includes the hidden fats in cheese, pastry, biscuits, nuts and fried foods.

The amount of fat we actually need is only about 5 g a day, so long as it contains the right kind of fatty acids. What are the right kinds of fatty acids?

Most of the 16 or so fatty acids and the glycerol we need to make up the various parts of the body can be made by the body itself from carbohydrates and proteins. But the fatty acids known as the 'essential' fatty acids cannot be made at all, or not in sufficient amounts. So we have to eat them in foods. These essential fatty acids are polyunsaturated and are called linoleic, linolenic and arachidonic acids.

So far as we know at the moment, so long as we get about 5 g of these essential fatty acids each day the body will have enough, and it can make the rest of the fats that are under the skin, around the kidneys and so on from other food components. All the talk about polyunsaturated fats, cholesterol and heart attacks will be discussed later.

The most important food sources of polyunsaturated fatty acids are some of the margarines, oily fish, and some vegetable oils such as corn, sunflower and safflower seed. But don't be persuaded that all vegetable oils are polyunsaturated. Palm oil, which is widely used in the less expensive liquid oils, is very saturated, and so is coconut oil.

The amount of fat we need is extremely small compared with the amount we currently eat. It's so small that it is almost impossible for anyone to eat so little or to suffer from a deficiency of essential fatty acids. It was only when people began to be fed intravenously that we realised what the symptoms of EFA deficiency are. Clearly, when nutrients are pumped straight into a vein, they have to be pre-digested synthetic mixtures of vitamins, minerals, amino acids (which make up proteins) and glucose. In the early days of intravenous feeding, when totally fat-free mixtures were used, some patients developed a kind of anaemia, their wounds did not heal well and fat was formed in the body and deposited in the liver.

It is not easy to see quite why these symptoms should occur, even when we look at the known functions of the essential fatty acids. They seem to be the starting blocks for the production by the body of a large group of compounds known as prostaglandins. These were discovered only recently and there is a great deal of work to do to find out precisely what each of them does. But already we know that they are responsible for affecting a whole range of activities such as body temperature regulation, blood clotting, stimulating the uterus to contract, and the production of pain sensation.

For everyone who eats normal foods, the distribution of essential fatty acids is such that it would be very difficult not to eat enough. In fact, if we ate only enough fat to supply the body's need for essential fatty acids, we would be eating an extremely low-fat diet.

Palatability Apart from giving us essential nutrients, fats also make food pleasant to eat. They improve the texture of foods and carry flavours. Many food flavours dissolve in fats much more readily than in the water component of foods. Just remember what happens to cream or milk when you leave them near a cut pineapple!

If you think of all your favourite foods, there's a good chance that a large number of them will be rather fatty. Fried fish and chips, doughnuts, chocolate, pastry pies, flans and croissants, nuts and cream are all delicious – and fatty! A low-fat diet does not mean you can never eat any of these. It means you can eat them all – but not too often. And it is getting the frequency right that this book is designed to help with.

The problems of too much fat It's only recently that people have been aware of the dangers of eating too much fat. And it must be said at the outset that we still don't know what the ideal fat level in the overall diet is. Up until a few decades ago, most nutrition text books said that the main function of both fats and carbohydrates was to supply energy for life and activity, and it didn't matter much what proportions of each you ate.

Since then we have become acutely aware of the numbers of people who have heart attacks, and of the increasing numbers who develop some kind of cancer. Investigators who tried to find the reasons for these disturbing facts looked, among other things, at the food we eat. Their observations revealed that groups of people who ate large amounts of fat had a high incidence of heart attacks and of some kinds of cancer. Conversely, they found that many groups who ate a low-fat diet had much less heart disease.

It would be all too easy to say that, from these observations, fat causes heart disease. Unfortunately that is by no means the logical conclusion. To find proof that something causes heart disease, we need to make many more investigations of different kinds. When diet has been changed to see if reducing fat does help reduce heart attacks, the results are sometimes encouraging, sometimes not.

At the present time what we can say is that heart disease seems to be caused by many factors – not least of which are smoking, not taking enough exercise and being too fat. So cutting out smoking and taking more exercise are definitely beneficial for the vast majority of people. And it seems to be a good idea to eat less fat too, because it's quite likely to do some good for all sorts of people. Not least, it will help to slim the overweight. And being slim reduces the risk of high blood pressure which itself is one of the factors linked with heart disease.

Saturated or polyunsaturated? This is the difficult question. Many people believe from what they have read in the press and in advertisements for some margarines that eating more polyunsaturated fats will help to ward off heart attacks. Unfortunately there is no proof that this is so. And simply eating more polyunsaturates won't do anything to reduce a thick waist.

From all the experiments that have been done, and from the observations that have been made, the best advice is to cut down on all kinds of fats, but especially on saturated fats like meat fat, palm oil, hard margarines, butter and cream, hard cheese and fatty foods. That doesn't mean eating none of these; it means eating small amounts. You'll see how small in a moment. If you use oils for cooking foods, make sure they are the polyunsaturated kind. If you want to use a polyunsaturated margarine, do so, but again, don't spread it thickly.

It's true that eating certain polyunsaturated fats does lower blood cholesterol levels. It's also true that eating lots of saturated fatty acids increases the amount of cholesterol in the blood. But there is no good evidence that manipulating blood cholesterol levels by altering diet in this way has any beneficial effects on the chance of having a heart attack.

The best we can say is that eating less fat is likely to do some good, but just relying on that is probably not enough. To reduce the risk of heart disease we need to eat a low-fat, high-fibre, diet throughout life, to take regular exercise that is vigorous enough to make us out of breath, and to stop smoking. Being the right body weight throughout life is important too.

High calorie fat When it comes to body weight, and the causes of overweight, we are on much more certain ground. There are only three factors which have any effect. The first you can't do anything about – the genes you inherited from your parents. If they dictate that you will gain weight if you overeat, then you'll have to pay attention to the kind and amount of food you eat. The people who don't gain weight no matter what they eat are in the minority!

The second factor is exercise and overall physical activity. There's no doubt that the more exercise you take, the more energy you use up.

And finally, of course, there's food. Quite simply, if you eat more calories than your body wants to keep it going, you're likely to store the remainder as body fat. Conversely, by eating fewer calories than your body wants, you will have to call on the stored reserves to supply the deficit. Fat will be removed from the body.

So the answer is obvious. Take more exercise and eat fewer calories.

Each gram of protein or sugar or starch gives you about 4 calories (16 kilojoules). A gram of alcohol contains 7 calories (29 kJ) and a gram of fat contains 9 calories (37 kJ). So it's pretty obvious that the most effective way of eating fewer calories is to eat less fat.

Get used to eating bread – wholemeal of course – with only the merest scraping of butter or margarine, or try low-fat curd cheese sometimes, or nothing at all. Reduce the amount of fried food you eat by using a non-stick frying pan. Trim all fat from the meat. Eat pastry only once a week and go very easy on cakes, biscuits, crisps, nuts and chocolate. You can see how high these foods are in fat, and therefore in calories, by looking at the chart on page 14.

How much fat? We've already seen that we *need* only a tiny amount of fat and that a diet that low in fat is very unpalatable. At present, a typical Western diet derives about 40% of its energy from fat. To help reduce the risk of heart attacks and some forms of cancer it is recommemded that only 30 to 35% of the energy should come from fat. That doesn't sound much of a change, but if you are used to eating fish and chips, pie and chips and jam doughnuts most days you will find the reduction rather large.

Putting that into amounts of fat for different groups of people means that a woman who did not want to lose weight would need to eat about 75 to 85 g of fat a day. The chart below gives an idea of the amount of fat that is recommended for men, women and children who do not need to lose weight.

A guide to daily fat and calorie intakes for a healthy diet

	FAT (g)	ENERGY Calories	kJ
Children 3–5	55–65	1600	6700
5–7	60–70	1800	7500
7–9	70–80	2100	8800
9–12	80–95	2400	10000
Teenage boys	100–115	2900	12100
Teenage girls	75–90	2300	9600
Women 18–55	75–85	2200	9200
over 55	65–75	2000	8400
Men 18–65	100–115	2900	12100
over 65	75–85	2200	9200

The figures in this table are only a rough guide to the kind of fat levels you should be aiming for. If you are very active you will need to eat more calories than are shown, and therefore some more fat. If you are trying to lose weight, women will be aiming for 1200 calories and 45 g of fat a day, and men for 1500 calories and 50 to 60 g of fat a day.

The low-fat diet in practice You'll see that most of the recipes in this book provide only a small proportion of the daily fat requirement for the low-fat diet. But remember that milk, butter and snacks are not included. You'll be eating these, so use the chart on page 14 to get an idea of the total amount of fat you are eating in a day.

Another advantage of the low-fat diet is that it's bulky. You'll be eating a fair amount of potato, rice, fruits and vegetables because these things are very low in fat. They are also quite high in water and water doesn't contain a single calorie. So there may well be a large volume of food on the dinner plate, but it still won't be high in fat. And, providing you don't go mad on bread and other low-fat foods, you'll be able to control calorie intake very easily and not feel hungry. So, the low-fat diet is a healthy one not only because of the reduction in fat but also because it is high in dietary fibre.

Finally, try to stick to three meals a day with nothing in between. If you have to eat something at mid-morning or mid-afternoon, make it fruit or bread – not fruit salad and cream, or bread and butter!

A guide to fat contents of different food portions

	AMOUNT	WEIGHT (g)	FAT (g)	ENERGY Calories	kJ
All Bran	5 tbsp	50	3	135	580
Almonds	18	25	13	140	580
Apple	1	125	0	50	210
Apricots, fresh	2	100	0	30	120
Avocado pear flesh	$\frac{1}{2}$	50	11	110	460
Bacon, streaky, grilled	2 rashers	25	9	90	370
Baked beans	sm. can	150	1	110	460
Banana	1 large	125	0	90	420
Beef: roast, lean	2 sm. sl.	75	3	120	490
roast, lean & fat	2 sm. sl.	90	11	190	800
minced, raw		75	12	165	690
Beer	1 pint		0	180	750
Biscuits:					
digestive	2	25	5	115	500
cream crackers	2	15	2	60	260
shortbread	1	25	7	200	830
Bread: white	1 med. sl.	40	1	95	400
wholemeal	1 med. sl.	40	1	85	370
Broad beans		50	0	25	100
Broccoli, boiled		75	0	15	60
Brussels sprouts	8	75	0	15	60
Butter	1 level tbsp	15	12	110	460
Cabbage, boiled		75	0	10	40
Carrots, boiled		75	0	15	60
Cake: fruit	1 sm. sl.	75	8	250	1050
sponge/cream	1 sm. sl.	50	9	200	830
Cauliflower, boiled		75	0	8	35
Cheese: Cheddar		50	16	200	840
cottage	sm. tub	110	5	110	460
Edam		50	11	150	630
Stilton		50	20	230	960
cream	3 level tbsp	50	23	220	900
curd	3 level tbsp	50	5	70	290
Chicken: no skin	1 portion	200	6	160	700
roast meat & skin	3 slices	75	11	160	680
Chocolate, milk	sm. bar	50	15	260	1110
Cod: fillet		120	0	90	390
in batter	1 piece	110	10	200	830
Corned beef	3 thin sl.	50	6	110	460
Cornflakes	6 tbsp	20	0	75	310
Cream: double	2 tbsp	30	14	135	550
whipping	2 tbsp	30	11	100	420
single	2 tbsp	30	6	65	260
Cornish pasty	1	200	40	660	2800
Currants, dried	2 tbsp	40	0	110	460

	AMOUNT	WEIGHT (g)	FAT (g)	ENERGY Calories	kJ
Doughnut	1	50	8	170	730
Egg: boiled	1	60	6	90	370
fried	1	60	10	140	580
Fishcake, fried	1 small	60	6	110	470
Gammon, lean, grilled	1 steak	110	6	190	800
Gin	1 single	25	0	55	230
Grapefruit	$\frac{1}{2}$ large	100	0	20	90
Hazelnuts	15	15	5	60	230
Herring, grilled, whole	1	150	13	200	840
Honey	1 tbsp	15	0	45	180
Ice cream	2 scoops	100	8	160	700
Jam	1 tbsp	15	0	40	170
Kidney, lamb's	1	50	1	45	190
Kipper fillet	1	50	5	100	430
Lamb: roast, lean	2 sm. sl.	75	6	140	600
roast, lean & fat	2 sm. sl.	90	16	240	1000
chop, lean & fat	1 with bone	150	33	410	1720
Liver, fried	3 sm. sl.	75	10	190	800
Liver sausage		50	13	150	640
Low-fat spread	1 level tbsp	15	6	55	230
Macaroni, boiled		100	0	120	500
Margarine	1 level tbsp	15	12	110	450
Mayonnaise	1 level tbsp	15	12	110	440
Milk: whole	300 ml/$\frac{1}{2}$ pint		11	190	770
skimmed	300 ml/$\frac{1}{2}$ pint		1	95	400
Mushrooms, fried	10 small	50	11	100	430
Oatmeal	4 tbsp	20	2	80	340
Olives	5	25	3	25	100
Oil	1 tbsp	15	15	135	555
Orange, whole	1	200	0	50	220
Parsnips, boiled	$\frac{1}{2}$ large	75	0	40	180
Pastry, cooked	2 tart cases	40	12	225	940
Peach	1	110	0	40	150
Peanuts		25	12	140	590
Pear	1	150	0	45	170
Peas, boiled	4 hpd. tbsp	50	0	25	110
Pork: roast, lean	2 sm. sl.	75	5	140	580
roast, lean & fat	2 sm. sl.	90	18	260	1070
chop, lean & fat	1 with bone	150	28	200	1610
Potato: boiled	1 medium	200	0	180	750
roast	1 small	100	5	160	660
chips		100	11	250	1070
crisps	sm. packet	25	9	130	560
Prawns, cooked		75	1	60	250
Prunes	6	dry-50	0	60	250
Rice, boiled	6 hpd. tbsp	90	0	110	470
Sausage, grilled	1 large	40	10	125	530

	AMOUNT	WEIGHT (g)	FAT (g)	ENERGY Calories	kJ
Scampi in breadcrumbs, fried		100	18	320	1320
Sugar	1 level tbsp	15	0	60	250
Salmon steak	1	100	11	160	670
Sardines in tomato sauce	2	50	6	90	370
Trout, whole, grilled	1	200	6	180	750
Weetabix	2	35	1	120	500
Wine	1 glass	150	0	100	420
Yogurt, natural low-fat	sm. tub	150	1	75	320
Yogurt, low-fat fruit	sm. tub	150	1	140	610

Starters

Set the standard for the meal to follow with any of these unusual and appetising openers. Tiny button mushrooms cooked in cider, savoury stuffed peppers or tomatoes and a genuine Norwegian recipe for home-cured salmon, are just some of the starters that would make equally delicious light luncheon or supper dishes.

Mushrooms en Cocotte

(Illustrated on page 33)

Per portion: 1 g fat   80 calories/330 kJ

450 g/1 lb button mushrooms
1 tablespoon vegetable oil
4 tablespoons stock
1 heaped tablespoon flour

300 ml/½ pint cider
salt and freshly ground black pepper
2 tablespoons fresh breadcrumbs
parsley sprigs to garnish

Grease four individual ovenproof ramekins.

Sauté the mushrooms for a few minutes in the oil and stock, then drain. Sprinkle on the flour and mix in gently. Add the cider slowly, mixing all together, and bring to the boil, stirring. Season to taste. Spoon into the ramekins and sprinkle over the breadcrumbs. Toast to a golden brown under the grill. Serve, garnished with parsley. *Serves 4*

Grapefruit-watercress cocktail

Per portion: 1 g fat   85 calories/360 kJ

600 ml/1 pint grapefruit juice
300 ml/½ pint watercress leaves
juice of ½ lemon
1 tablespoon runny honey

600 ml/1 pint low-fat natural yogurt
GARNISH
½ lemon, sliced
watercress sprigs

Pour the grapefruit juice into the blender goblet. Add the watercress leaves, lemon juice, honey and yogurt and liquidise at high speed. Transfer to individual glasses and garnish each with a slice of lemon and a sprig of watercress. *Serves 6*

Tomates Farcies Duxelles

Per portion: 9 g fat   190 calories/800 kJ

6 medium-sized mushrooms
1 shallot or small onion
1 stick celery
65 g/2½ oz butter or margarine
STOCK
1 teaspoon chopped basil or ½
  teaspoon dried basil
1 tablespoon chopped parsley

½ teaspoon chopped lemon thyme
4 tablespoons fresh white
  breadcrumbs
salt and freshly ground black pepper
6 firm tomatoes
1 small clove garlic, crushed
6 rounds toast
parsley sprigs to garnish

Clean and peel the mushrooms and remove stalks. Chop peelings and stalks finely and keep on one side. Finely chop the shallot or onion and celery. Heat 15 g/½ oz of the butter or margarine and cook the shallot and celery very slowly. Add the duxelles (mushroom peelings and stalks) and continue to cook over a low heat until everything is soft (about 7 minutes). Add a little stock if necessary. Add the herbs and breadcrumbs and continue cooking, turning everything about in the pan, until the breadcrumbs have begun to brown. Season to taste.

Cut the tops off the tomatoes and scoop out the seeds and juice; drain the tomatoes upside down for a minute. Fry the mushroom caps in 15 g/½ oz of the butter or margarine. Stuff the tomatoes with the breadcrumb mixture and top each with a fried mushroom cap. Work the crushed garlic into the remaining butter or margarine, then spread it on the rounds of toasted bread. Place one stuffed tomato on each round of toast. Cover with greased foil and bake in a hot oven (220 C, 425 F, gas 7) for 10 minutes. Garnish with parsley. *Serves 6*

Smoked Fish

Good Scotch smoked salmon is always delicious, and a great compliment to your guests, but it is very expensive now, so it is worth experimenting with some of the other varieties of smoked fish. Smoked trout is served with horseradish, and smoked mackerel and buckling are cheaper and both good. Smoked eels are some people's passion – but they are very much a matter of personal taste.

Serve smoked fish with a selection of the following: brown bread, lemon wedges, horseradish sauce and lettuce hearts.

Fresh Tomato Juice Cocktail

A really refreshing starter. Make this when tomatoes are plentiful.

Per portion: 0 g fat   35 calories/150 kJ

1.75 kg/4 lb ripe tomatoes
1 teaspoon sugar
juice of 1 small lemon
good twist of lemon peel
2 teaspoons Worcestershire sauce
3 drops Tabasco sauce

1 teaspoon salt
freshly ground black pepper
GARNISH
lemon slices
watercress sprigs

Roughly chop the tomatoes. Place in the liquidiser with the sugar. Blend and sieve. Pour the juice into a glass jug with the remaining ingredients and chill for several hours, for the lemon peel to infuse its flavour.

Pour into individual glasses and garnish each with a lemon slice and small sprig of watercress. *Serves 8*

Melon with Vermouth

(Illustrated on page 33)

Per portion: 0 g fat   110 calories/450 kJ

1 small melon
4 oranges, segmented
4 tablespoons white vermouth

1 egg white
caster sugar
4 sprigs mint

Scoop out the flesh from the melon with a small ball cutter. Place in a bowl with the orange segments (free from pith or membrane) and pour over the vermouth. Cover and chill.

Dip the rims of four glasses first into the lightly whisked egg white, then into caster sugar, to make a pretty frosted rim. To serve, turn the melon mixture into the prepared glasses and garnish each with a mint sprig. *Serves 4*

Tagliatelle Romana

My version of a marvellous pasta dish served in a little Roman restaurant.

Per portion: 1 g fat   320 calories/1340 kJ

225 g/8 oz tagliatelle noodles
chicken stock
50 g/2 oz smoked prosciutto ham

100 g/4 oz Soft Curd Cheese (page 104)
1 clove garlic, crushed
salt and freshly ground black pepper

Cook the tagliatelle in plenty of chicken stock until just tender, then drain and turn into a hot dish.

Remove any fat from the prosciutto and cut the meat into strips. Sieve the curd cheese and mix in the garlic and seasoning. Stir the cheese mixture into the tagliatelle, toss in the ham strips and serve immediately. *Serves 4*

Gravad Lax

This is my Norwegian mother-in-law's recipe for home-cured salmon, which in Norway is considered more of a delicacy than smoked salmon. If you are economising, buy the tailpiece of the salmon, and negotiate a good price with your fishmonger. A fresh mackerel is also excellent treated in the same way, head removed and filleted.

Per portion: 15 g fat   230 calories/900 kJ

1 kg/2 lb piece of salmon, or 1 large mackerel
juice of 1 small lemon
FOR THE MIXTURE
1 heaped tablespoon salt
1 heaped tablespoon caster sugar

1 tablespoon crushed black peppercorns
2 heaped tablespoons chopped dill
GARNISH
lemon wedges
chopped dill

Mix together the ingredients for the mixture. Lay a large piece of cling film or foil on a plate and spread on a quarter of this mixture, to an area the size of the fish. Over it lay the opened-out fish, skin side down. Remove any remaining fish bones then spread over half the mixture. Fold to make a fish shape again, and spread the remaining quarter of the mixture on top. Close up the cling film or foil and seal to make a neat parcel. Cover with a weight on a board.

Leave in the refrigerator for 3–4 days, turning the parcel twice a day. Unwrap and drain. Sprinkle with the lemon juice. Serve, in thin slices, with lemon wedges and chopped dill, and plenty of brown bread and butter or margarine.

Note: This dish freezes well. Drain thoroughly and wrap in fresh cling film, then aluminium foil. *Serves 8*

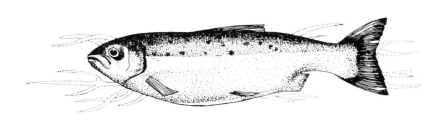

Stuffed Green Peppers

Per portion: 1 g fat   120 calories/500 kJ

6 green peppers
175 g/6 oz long-grain rice
salt
rind and juice of 1 large lemon

3 tablespoons chopped herbs
  (parsley, chives and thyme)
150 ml/$\frac{1}{4}$ pint oil-free French
  dressing

Slice off and reserve the lids of the peppers and carefully remove all seeds and pith from inside. Wash the pepper and blanch for 6 minutes in boiling water, then plunge immediately into cold water, to keep the fresh colour. Drain and pat dry with absorbent kitchen paper.

Boil the rice in plenty of salted water for 10 minutes. Drain and cool. Flavour the rice with the grated lemon rind and juice and chopped herbs. Toss with a little French dressing and pile into the peppers. Replace the pepper lids. Finally, pour a little more French dressing over the peppers and serve. *Serves 6*

Eggs Florentine

Per Portion: 11 g fat   250 calories/1050 kJ

675 g/1$\frac{1}{2}$ lb fresh leaf spinach
$\frac{1}{2}$ teaspoon sugar
salt and pepper
15 g/$\frac{1}{2}$ oz butter or margarine

4 eggs
2 tablespoons grated Parmesan
  cheese
450 ml/$\frac{3}{4}$ pint low-fat natural yogurt

Wash the spinach carefully and cook with the sugar and just a little water. Drain, press well and season to taste. Place in a heated gratin dish, dot with butter or margarine and make four hollows. Poach the eggs and lay one in each of the hollowed nests. Meanwhile, mix half the cheese with the yogurt and warm through. Spoon the yogurt over the eggs and spinach and sprinkle the remaining cheese on top. Flash under a hot grill to melt the cheese and serve at once. *Serves 4*

Port of Spain Prawns

(Illustrated on page 33)

This is a recipe from Trinidad.

Per portion: **1 g fat**   **100 calories/420 kJ**

2 very small pineapples
4 tablespoons peeled and diced
  cucumber
½ teaspoon salt
½ teaspoon ground cumin
½ teaspoon ground coriander
freshly ground black pepper

100 g/4 oz peeled prawns
150 ml/¼ pint thick low-fat natural
  yogurt
GARNISH
4 unpeeled prawns
4 sprigs watercress or mint

Halve the pineapples and remove the cores. Scoop out the flesh, chop it and put in a bowl. Reserve the pineapple shells. Sprinkle the cucumber with the salt and drain in a colander for about 30 minutes. Pat dry. Mix the cumin, coriander, pepper and yogurt together. Add the cucumber to the pineapple and combine with the peeled prawns and the yogurt.

Pile into the pineapple shells and garnish with an unpeeled prawn and a sprig of watercress or mint. Serve with brown bread. *Serves 4*

Les Crudités

A collection of small raw vegetables and salads assembled in groups
on a serving dish, with bowls of different sauces to accompany
them.

Radishes, baby tomatoes, florets of cauliflower, sticks of celery and carrot, strips of sweet pepper, rounds of raw courgettes, endive leaves, baby beetroot (cooked), watercress sprigs, quartered hard-boiled eggs and tiny new potatoes are all suitable. Wash and dry them and arrange in groups in an attractive design on a chilled serving dish.

Each guest should have a plate and also a finger bowl filled with warm water and a slice of lemon; rose petals add a touch of luxury. The vegetables are eaten with the fingers. Serve at least three sauces, in separate bowls; anchovy sauce, mustard sauce and garlic sauce would be lovely (see pages 96, 99 and 100). Pass a basket of hot crusty bread, sea salt and a pepper mill. *Serves 6–9*

Soups

Warming winter soups, simple summer soups, various vegetable soups and even exotic soups. As a way of bringing out the true flavour of fresh vegetables, or turning an assortment of ingredients into a tempting, wholesome dish, soups are unbeatable.

Walnut Soup

Per portion: 10 g fat 110 calories/460 kJ

100 g/4 oz shelled walnuts
1 clove garlic, crushed
900 ml/1½ pints hot chicken stock,
  made with 2 stock cubes

salt and white pepper
150 ml/¼ pint low-fat natural yogurt
watercress sprigs to garnish

Put the walnuts and garlic into the liquidiser with a little stock and blend to
a creamy consistency. Turn into a saucepan, gradually stir in the remaining
stock and heat through. Season to taste.

Remove from the heat and stir in the yogurt. Serve, garnished with small
sprigs of watercress. *Serves 6*

Italian Leek and Pumpkin Soup

The hollowed-out shell of the pumpkin can be used as a tureen for this soup.

Per portion: 2 g fat 100 calories/420 kJ

1 Spanish onion, chopped
50 g/2 oz chopped leek
2 tablespoons stock
450 g/1 lb pumpkin flesh
225 g/8 oz potatoes
salt and freshly ground black pepper

600 ml/1 pint skimmed milk
600 ml/1 pint hot chicken stock
100 g/4 oz cooked long-grain rice
150 ml/¼ pint low-fat natural yogurt
chopped parsley to garnish

Soften the onion and leek in the stock. Dice the pumpkin flesh and potatoes
and add, with the seasoning, milk and stock, to the onions. Bring to the boil,
cover and simmer for 45 minutes, stirring frequently.

Blend the soup in the liquidiser or press through a sieve. Return to the pan
and add the cooked rice and most of the yogurt. Reheat gently. Serve,
topped with the remaining yogurt and sprinkled with parsley. *Serves 8*

Country Vegetable Soup

Per portion: 4 g fat   110 calories/460 kJ

1 small onion, chopped
2 leeks, washed, trimmed and sliced
3 sticks celery, sliced
25 g/1 oz butter or margarine
350 g/12 oz ripe tomatoes, peeled
   and chopped

generous litre/2 pints light chicken
   or vegetable stock
225 g/8 oz potatoes, sliced
1 clove garlic, chopped
salt and pepper
pinch of cayenne

Soften the onion, leeks and celery in the butter or margarine but do not brown. Add the tomatoes and stock, then the potatoes and garlic. Bring to the boil, stirring occasionally. Cover and simmer for about 30 minutes, until the vegetables are tender. Sieve or blend in the liquidiser until smooth; if the soup seems too thick, add a little more stock.

Return to the pan, reheat and adjust for seasoning. Add a pinch of cayenne to serve. *Serves 6*

27

Spinach Soup

(Illustrated on page 52)

Per portion: 4 g fat   95 calories/400kJ

1 small onion, chopped
15 g/½ oz butter or margarine
1 tablespoon flour

225 g/8 oz finely chopped frozen
   spinach, defrosted
600 ml/1 pint chicken or veal stock
150 ml/¼ pint low-fat natural yogurt

Soften the onion in the butter or margarine. Stir in the flour and cook for 1 minute. Stir in the spinach and cook over low heat for 3 minutes, stirring. Add the stock, bring to the boil, cover and simmer gently for 10 minutes.
   Just before serving, remove from the heat and stir in the yogurt, or pour a little over each serving if you prefer. *Serves 4*

Courgette and Cucumber Soup

Per portion: 0 g fat   25 calories/100 kJ

1 cucumber, roughly chopped
equal weight in courgettes, chopped

900 ml/1½ pints chicken stock
snipped chives to garnish

Simmer the cucumber and courgettes in the stock for 15 minutes. Blend in the liquidiser or press through a sieve. Reheat or serve chilled, garnished with a pinch of chives. *Serves 4*

Iced Cucumber Soup

Per portion: 3 g fat   110 calories/460 kJ

1 small onion, finely chopped
1 tablespoon vegetable oil
1 large cucumber, peeled and sliced
4 medium-sized potatoes, sliced

900 ml/1½ pints light chicken stock
salt and white pepper
2 tablespoons low-fat natural yogurt
chopped mint to garnish

Soften the onion in the oil, then add the cucumber and potato. Cook very gently for 10 minutes, stirring from time to time, without browning. Add the stock and bring to the boil. Cover and simmer gently for 20 minutes (not more).

Press through a sieve or blend in the liquidiser and pour into a bowl to cool. Adjust seasoning when the soup is cold. Just before serving, stir in the yogurt and garnish with chopped mint. Serve chilled, with hot crusty rolls.
Serves 6

Carrot and Tomato Soup

Per portion: 2 g fat   65 calories/270 kJ

15 g/½ oz butter or margarine
1 medium-sized onion, chopped
1 kg/2 lb ripe tomatoes, chopped
225 g/8 oz carrots, grated
scant 1.5 litres/2½ pints light chicken
    or vegetable stock

2 sugar cubes
2 oranges
6 peppercorns
small bay leaf
1 clove
salt and pepper

Heat the butter or margarine in a large heavy-bottomed pan. Add the onion, cover and cook gently for a few minutes. Add the tomatoes and carrots and cook slowly, still covered, for about 10 minutes, stirring occasionally; add a little stock if necessary. Rub the sugar cubes over the oranges to absorb the flavour, then add to the pan with the remaining stock. Bring to the boil, cover and simmer for 20 minutes.

Give it a quick jizz in the liquidiser, then sieve the soup into a clean pan. Stir in the juice squeezed from the oranges, the peppercorns, bay leaf and clove. Leave these last three ingredients to infuse for about 1 hour if possible, then remove. Taste and adjust for seasoning. Heat through and strain into a hot tureen to serve. *Serves 8*

Vichyssoise

This is an elegant chilled soup, an ideal starter for a summer dinner party. Served hot, with skimmed milk in place of the yogurt, it becomes Potage Bonne Femme, a comforting and delicious winter soup.

Per portion: 0 g fat   140 calories/580 kJ

4 large leeks
1 small onion, chopped
600 ml/1 pint chicken stock
4 medium-sized potatoes, sliced

salt and white pepper
150 ml/$\frac{1}{4}$ pint low-fat natural yogurt
snipped chives to garnish

Wash, trim and chop the leeks. Soften with the onion in a little of the stock. Add the potatoes and cook gently for a further 5 minutes. Pour in the remaining stock and season to taste. Bring to the boil, cover and simmer for 20 minutes. Press through a sieve or blend in the liquidiser. Cool and stir in the yogurt.

Serve chilled, sprinkled with chives. *Serves 6*

French Onion Soup

(Illustrated on page 34)

Per portion: 4 g fat   225 calories/950 kJ

3 large Spanish onions, finely
  chopped
generous litre/2 pints beef stock,
  made with 2 stock cubes
1 teaspoon sugar
salt and freshly ground black pepper

6 slices French bread
100 g/4 oz Edam cheese, grated
1 tablespoon brandy
chopped parsley to garnish
  (optional)

Cook the onions in some of the stock, in a thick-bottomed covered pan, for at least 30 minutes, turning frequently. They should not brown but should be quite soft. Add the rest of the stock, the sugar, salt and pepper, and boil for a further 30 minutes.

Meanwhile, toast the bread slices in the oven, heap the grated cheese on top and brown under the grill. Now stir the brandy into the soup and serve, with a cheesy bread slice in each bowl. Sprinkle with chopped parsley, if liked. *Serves 6*

Winter Vegetable Soup

Per portion: 1 g fat   40 calories/170 kJ

225 g/8 oz carrots, chopped
225 g/8 oz parsnips, chopped
175 g/6 oz turnips, chopped
175 g/6 oz swede, chopped

generous litre/2 pints chicken or
  beef stock, made with 2 stock
  cubes
2 tablespoons chopped parsley
salt and freshly ground black pepper

Cook all the chopped vegetables in the stock for 25–30 minutes, until tender. Add the parsley and season to taste. *Serves 6*

FROM THE TOP: *Melon with Vermouth (page 21); Port of Spain Prawns (page 24); Mushrooms en Cocotte (page 18)*

Artichoke Soup

Per portion: 3 g fat   100 calories/420 kJ

450 g/1 lb Jerusalem artichokes
1 tablespoon vegetable oil
generous litre/2 pints skimmed milk

salt and white pepper
chopped parsley to garnish

Carefully scrape and chop the artichokes. Cook gently in the oil in a heavy-bottomed saucepan, stirring frequently, until soft. Add a little milk if the artichokes start to turn brown. When soft, blend the artichokes in the liquidiser with some of the milk or press them through a sieve. Return the purée to the saucepan, stir in the remaining milk and bring to the boil. Cover and simmer for 10 minutes. Taste and adjust for seasoning and sprinkle over chopped parsley. *Serves 6*

Fresh Tomato Soup

(Illustrated on page 70)

The simplest and best method I know.

Per portion: 2 g fat   50 calories/200 kJ

1 kg/2 lb ripe tomatoes, roughly
   chopped
1 small onion, chopped
1 tablespoon vegetable oil
1 sugar cube

1 orange
1.75 litres/3 pints light stock
   (chicken, turkey or veal)
2 cloves
bouquet garni

Soften the tomatoes and onion in the oil for about 8 minutes. Rub the sugar cube over the orange peel, to absorb the zest, and add with the remaining ingredients to the tomato mixture. Bring to the boil, cover and simmer gently for 25 minutes. Remove the cloves and bouquet garni.

Blend the soup in a liquidiser then push with a wooden spoon through a fine sieve. Reheat and serve.

The subtle orange flavour really does make all the difference to this delicious soup. *Serves 8*

FROM THE TOP: *French Onion Soup (page 32); Portuguese Cod (page 42); Pancakes St. Clements (page 115)*

Gazpacho

(Illustrated on page 87)

A Spanish favourite.

Per portion: 6 g fat   100 calories/420 kJ

4 large ripe tomatoes, peeled and
  deseeded
½ Spanish onion, sliced
2 small green peppers, deseeded and
  chopped
1 cucumber, diced
450 ml/¾ pint tomato juice
1 clove garlic, chopped
3 tablespoons olive or corn oil
4 tablespoons lemon juice

salt and freshly ground black pepper
1 teaspoon sugar
8 ice cubes
GARNISH
2 slices bread, diced
2 tomatoes, peeled and quartered
diced green pepper
diced cucumber
½ Spanish onion

Blend in the liquidiser the tomatoes, onion, peppers (keeping some aside for the garnish), cucumber (keeping some for garnish), tomato juice, garlic, oil, lemon juice, seasoning and sugar. Chill. Just before serving, add the ice cubes.

Accompany the large bowl of gazpacho with small bowls of toasted diced bread, tomatoes and green pepper, cucumber and onion rings. *Serves 8*

Fish

Cooking in a brick is one way of cooking fish to perfection. But not the only way. Try mackerel with yogurt and chives, a Norwegian dish, deceptively simple and quite delicious; or psari plaki, fish baked in the oven with oil and herbs, the Greek way. Kedgeree, fish pie and trout with almonds are already favourites and need no recommendation – and don't forget that fish is a wonderfully nourishing food for anyone on a low-fat diet.

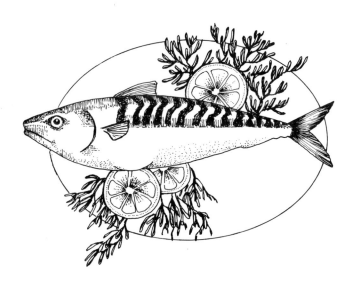

Fish in a Brick

One of the Venetian ways of preparing fish is to bake them in earthenware in the oven, with oil and herbs and lemon, and then to serve them cold, with more herbs and lemon. Mackerel, red mullet or grey mullet are suitable fish.

Per portion: 16 g fat   220 calories/920 kJ

1 large fish, cleaned
bay leaf, crumbled
2 teaspoons finely chopped parsley
2 teaspoons finely chopped thyme or
  fennel leaves

1 lemon, sliced
1 clove garlic, crushed
salt and freshly ground black pepper
vegetable oil

First soak a fish brick in cold water for 10 minutes. Remove.

Make a few incisions in the uppermost side of the fish. Mix together the herbs, lemon slices, garlic and seasoning. Sprinkle half this mixture inside the fish and over the cuts. Rub the underside with a little oil. Lay the fish in the brick and replace the cover. Put the brick into a cold oven and set the oven to moderately hot (190 C, 375 F, gas 5). Cook for about 1 hour. Allow the fish to cool and serve with the remaining herb mixture sprinkled over.

A potato salad and a tomato salad would accompany this well.

Note If you do not have a fish brick, the fish can be cooked successfully wrapped in foil in a roasting tin. *Serves 2*

Mackerel with Lemon and Bay Leaves

Per portion: 33 g fat   480 calories/2000 kJ

4 mackerel, cleaned and heads
   removed
seasoned flour to coat
2 large Spanish onions, sliced

1 lemon, thinly sliced
2 bay leaves, crumbled
1 teaspoon vegetable oil
salt and freshly ground black pepper

Coat the mackerel in seasoned flour and grill on each side until cooked through. Transfer to a heated serving dish and keep warm. Cook the onions, lemon slices and bay leaves in the oil until soft. Season to taste. Spoon over the fish and serve.

Mackerel must always be utterly fresh, with bright eyes and a sparkling silver body. Ask your fishmonger to clean the fish for you, and to remove the heads. *Serves 4*

Mackerel with Yogurt and Chives

A Norwegian dish.

Per portion: 32 g fat   500 calories/2100 kJ

4 mackerel, filleted
2 tablespoons seasoned flour

300 ml/½ pint low-fat natural yogurt
3 tablespoons snipped chives

Dust the mackerel fillets with the seasoned flour and grill on each side until cooked through. Heat the mixed yogurt and chives gently, and pour over the mackerel fillets. Serve at once, with plain boiled potatoes. As simple as it is delicious. *Serves 4*

Psari Plaki

Bream baked in the oven. A Greek dish.

Per portion: 3 g fat   330 calories/1380 kJ

1 tablespoon vegetable oil
2 onions, sliced
450 g/1 lb potatoes, sliced
2 carrots, sliced
2 sticks celery, chopped
225 g/8 oz tomatoes, peeled and
  chopped
stock

1 (1.5 to 1.75-kg/3 to 4-lb) bream,
  cut into steaks or divided into
  fillets
salt and freshly ground black pepper
juice of 1 lemon
2 teaspoons chopped lemon thyme
chopped parsley to garnish

Heat the oil in a sauté pan and add the onions. Cook gently for a few moments, then add the remaining vegetables in the order given. Cook, stirring occasionally, for about 10 minutes, until softened. Add a little stock if necessary.

Lay the fish steaks or fillets in a large oiled roasting dish. Sprinkle with salt and pepper and pour over the lemon juice. Scatter the chopped lemon thyme over the fish and surround with the vegetables. Pour the oil from the pan over the fish and vegetables. Cover with foil and bake in a moderately hot oven (200 C, 400 F, gas 6) for 40–50 minutes, or until the fish is cooked, basting from time to time. Serve sprinkled with parsley. *Serves 6*

Trout with Almonds

A popular way of cooking trout in England and Scandinavia, where the lovely fresh fish is in need of no further adornment.

Per portion: 6 g fat   240 calories/1000 kJ

6 trout, cleaned and heads removed
seasoned flour to coat
1 tablespoon vegetable oil

50 g/2 oz flaked almonds
lemon wedges to garnish

Coat the trout in seasoned flour and brush with oil. Grill the fish for 3–4 minutes on each side. Meanwhile, gently grill the almonds until golden on both sides.

Serve the trout scattered with the almonds and surrounded by lemon wedges. *Serves 6*

Plaice with Mushrooms and Cider

Per portion: 1 g fat 300 calories/1250 kJ

8 (50-g/2-oz) frozen plaice fillets
salt and white pepper
450 ml/¾ pint dry cider
450 g/1 lb button mushrooms
2 tablespoons stock

3 tablespoons flour
450 g/1 lb potatoes, cooked
skimmed milk
parsley sprig to garnish

Allow the fish fillets to thaw to room temperature. Season with salt and pepper, fold up each into three and lay in a sauté pan. Pour in the cider. Bring slowly to the boil, cover and cook for 10 minutes over very gentle heat.

Meanwhile, slice the mushrooms and cook until just soft in the stock. Sprinkle on the flour and mix in carefully until absorbed. Strain the cider liquor from the fish into a bowl and then add it slowly to the mushrooms, stirring. Cook for a few minutes, stirring all the time until the sauce thickens.

Arrange the plaice fillets on a hot serving dish and pour over the mushroom and cider sauce. Cream the potatoes with seasoning and a little skimmed milk, pipe a border round the fish and brown under the grill. Garnish with a sprig of parsley and serve with a mixed green salad. *Serves 4*

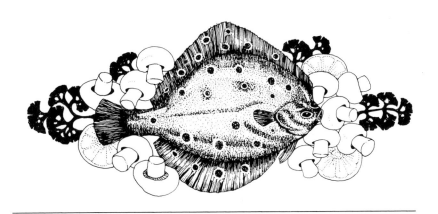

Portuguese Cod

(Illustrated on page 34)

Per portion: 5 g fat   230 calories/960 kJ

1 onion	juice of 1 lemon
25 g/1 oz butter or margarine	salt and freshly ground black pepper
1 clove garlic	4 (200-g/7-oz) cod steaks
4 tomatoes	chopped parsley to garnish

Peel and chop the onion and peel and crush the clove of garlic. Peel and chop the tomatoes.

Soften the chopped onion in the butter or margarine, over medium heat, without allowing it to brown. Add the crushed garlic, chopped tomatoes and lemon juice. Season to taste with salt and freshly ground black pepper and stir well.

Spoon about one-third of this sauce into a shallow ovenproof dish. Arrange the cod steaks on top, then pour over the remaining sauce. Cover the dish with a lid or with aluminium foil and bake in a moderately hot oven (190 C, 375 F, gas 5) for 25–30 minutes.

Remove from the oven and sprinkle over a little chopped parsley to garnish before serving. *Serves 4*

Kedgeree

Per portion: 1 g fat   300 calories/1250 kJ

450 g/1 lb smoked haddock, soaked
  in cold water
1 small onion, finely chopped
2 tablespoons stock
½ teaspoon curry powder
225 g/8 oz long-grain rice

salt and freshly ground black pepper
bay leaf
juice of 1 lemon
3 tablespoons chopped parsley
lemon wedges to serve

Bring the haddock barely to the boil in fresh water and simmer for a few minutes until tender. Drain and flake. Cook the onion in the stock until soft then sprinkle over the curry powder and cook for a minute longer.

Meanwhile, cook the rice in plenty of boiling salted water, with the bay leaf, for 10 minutes. Drain and sprinkle over a few drops of cold water to separate the grains and stop the rice cooking. Combine the flaked haddock, the onion mixture and the rice. Grind plenty of black pepper into the kedgeree and sprinkle over the lemon juice and parsley. Toss lightly and pile into a hot dish.

Serve with lemon wedges. *Serves 4*

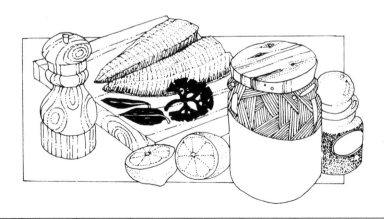

Salmon Mousse

Per portion: 8 g fat   175 calories/725 kJ

450 g/1 lb cold cooked salmon,
 flaked
15 g/½ oz butter or margarine
50 g/2 oz flour
300 ml/½ pint skimmed milk
salt and white pepper
tarragon sprig or bay leaf

15 g/½ oz powdered gelatine
2 tablespoons medium-dry sherry
3 egg whites, stiffly whisked
GARNISH
lettuce hearts or watercress sprigs
½ cucumber, thinly sliced

Pound the salmon in a bowl with the end of a rolling pin. Make a béchamel sauce (page 100) with the butter or margarine, flour, milk, seasoning and tarragon or bay leaf.

Soften the gelatine in the sherry, then dissolve it in a bowl over a saucepan of boiling water. Stir into the béchamel sauce and remove the tarragon sprig. Combine thoroughly with the salmon and fold in the stiffly whisked egg whites. Transfer to a lightly oiled 1.75-litre/3-pint soufflé dish and chill in the refrigerator until set.

To turn out, dip the dish quickly in a bowl of boiling water and run a knife around the inside edge. Invert on to a serving dish, surround with lettuce hearts or watercress sprigs and garnish with cucumber slices.

Because this is a fairly rich dish, the portions served should be modest. It makes an equally good starter for a special dinner party. *Serves 8*

Cold Salmon

For a very special occasion this, such as a small wedding reception or silver wedding anniversary party.

Per 100 g/4 oz portion: **12 g fat**   **180 calories/750 kJ**

1 salmon or salmon trout (not more than 4.5 kg/10 lb in weight)
FOR THE COURT BOUILLON
1 onion, sliced
½ lemon, sliced
bouquet garni
1 carrot, sliced
12 black peppercorns

GARNISH
½ cucumber, thinly sliced
18 unpeeled prawns
lettuce hearts
1 bunch watercress
mint leaves
6 tiny salmon pink roses, if available
2 lemons, sliced

Place sufficient water to cover the fish in a pan and add the ingredients for the court bouillon. Bring to the boil and simmer for 30 minutes. Cool.

Make sure that the inside of the fish is perfectly cleaned. Place the fish in a fish kettle in the *cold* court bouillon and cover. Bring very slowly to the boil, then boil for exactly 3 minutes. Remove from the heat and put the kettle in a cold place for at least 12 hours. However large your salmon this method will work, because a larger fish will take longer to cool down.

Lift out the fish on its drainer and slide gently on to a large dish. (I once used a plank of wood, cut to size and covered with foil, as a serving dish.) Skin the salmon carefully. Turn it over and skin the other side. Lay slices of cucumber down the entire centre length of the salmon. Peel the prawns, except for their heads (this looks prettier and leaves something firm to pick them up by) and lay them on the cucumber slices. Tuck tiny lettuce hearts round the salmon. Place a bunch of watercress where the head should be.

Put mint leaves and small salmon pink roses at each end of this really impressive dish – but do resist tomatoes, radishes or anything which might be a colour clash. Add fine curls of sliced lemon to your arrangement – but beware of gilding the lily! Serve with Cucumber Sauce (page 99).

Salmon Parcels

The paper parcels puff up in the oven and release a succulent smell when opened on the plate.

Per portion: 16 g fat   300 calories/1250 kJ

1 teaspoon onion juice
rind and juice of 1 lemon
4 tablespoons chopped parsley

1 tablespoon chopped fresh tarragon,
  or $\frac{1}{2}$ teaspoon dried
salt and freshly ground black pepper
4 individual salmon steaks

Mix the onion juice, grated lemon rind and juice, chopped parsley and chopped tarragon. Season to taste with salt and freshly ground black pepper.

Place each salmon steak on a sheet of non-stick baking paper. Divide the herb mixture into four and spoon one portion on top of each steak. Carefully fold and pleat the baking paper over each steak so that none of the juices can escape during cooking.

Place the parcels on a baking sheet and cook in a moderately hot oven (190 C, 375 F, gas 5) for 25–30 minutes.

Serve with plain boiled potatoes and a green vegetable or salad. *Serves 4*

Fish pie

Per portion: 6 g fat   300 calories/1250 kJ

675 g/1½ lb cod or haddock fillets, or
  a mixture of white fish
about 300 ml/½ pint skimmed milk
bay leaf
½ onion, sliced
6 peppercorns
40 g/1½ oz butter or margarine

3 tablespoons flour
salt and white pepper
2 tablespoons chopped parsley
4 tomatoes, peeled and sliced
1 kg/2 lb potatoes
150 ml/¼ pint hot skimmed milk

Simmer the fish gently in skimmed milk and water to cover, with the bay leaf, onion and peppercorns, until cooked. Measure off the fish liquor and make up to 450 ml/¾ pint with more skimmed milk if necessary.

Melt the butter or margarine and stir in the flour. Cook over gentle heat for 1 minute then stir in the strained fish liquor. Bring to the boil, stirring until the sauce is smooth and thick. Season to taste and stir in the chopped parsley. Pour a little sauce into a greased ovenproof dish and lay the fish over it. Top with the tomato slices and cover with the remaining sauce.

Meanwhile, cook the potatoes and beat to a purée with the hot skimmed milk. Season and pile on top of the fish mixture. Brown under the grill for a few minutes before serving. Green peas or a salad go well with this wholesome and popular family dish. *Serves 6*

Garlic and Tarragon Sauce for Steamed Fish

Total sauce recipe: **21 g fat**   **560 calories/2340 kJ**

300 ml/½ pint dry white wine
3 sprigs tarragon
25 g/1 oz butter or margarine
2 tablespoons flour

1 clove garlic, crushed
150 ml/¼ pint chicken stock
salt and freshly ground black pepper

To steam fish: place skinned fillets (folded in three) on a lightly oiled heatproof plate over a pan of boiling water. Invert another heatproof plate on top of the fish and cook over the steam for the required time. Meanwhile, make the sauce.

Reduce the wine by half, by fast boiling in an open pan. Add the chopped leaves of 2 tarragon sprigs and leave over a low heat until the scent of the herb is quite strong.

Melt the butter or margarine and stir in the flour. Cook for 1 minute, then add the garlic, stock and seasoning. Bring to the boil, stirring all the time until the sauce is smooth and thickened. Add the wine and tarragon mixture.

Just before serving, strain the sauce and add the remaining chopped tarragon leaves. *Makes 300 ml/½ pint*

Meat

As the recipes in this section show, low-fat cooking can be as tasty, imaginative and varied as you choose to make it. Whether a roast leg of lamb, pork in wine sauce, veal with Marsala or a casserole of beef, see how to cook these and many others, and without the added richness of cream, butter or eggs, you will rise from the table feeling replete and content, but still as lively as a cricket.

Porc aux Pruneaux

This is adapted from Curnonsky's Recettes des Provinces de France. The dish is made up of pork fillet, the prunes that are so exquisitely displayed in the shop windows in Tours, and the delicious wine of the Loire, Vouvray, which comes from nearby.

Per portion: 17 g fat   600 calories/2500 kJ

450 g/1 lb giant prunes
½ bottle Vouvray or medium-dry
   white wine
675 g/1½ lb pork fillet
2 tablespoons seasoned flour

25 g/1 oz butter or margarine
2 teaspoons redcurrant jelly
salt and freshly ground black pepper
300 ml/½ pint low-fat natural yogurt
parsley sprig to garnish

Soak the prunes overnight in the wine.

Cut the pork fillet into cubes and turn in the seasoned flour. Fry gently on all sides in the butter or margarine until golden and cooked through. Meanwhile, simmer the prunes for 30 minutes in the wine.

Drain the prunes, reserving the juice, and place them round the edge of a heated serving dish. Arrange the pork in the centre. Add the prune liquor to the meat juices in the frying pan, boil to reduce slightly and thicken, then stir in the redcurrant jelly until blended. Taste and adjust for seasoning. Carefully stir in half the yogurt and warm through. Pour over the pork, but not the prunes, and spoon over the remaining yogurt. Garnish with parsley and serve with a watercress and tomato salad. *Serves 4*

FROM THE TOP: *Compote of Rhubarb (page 112); Porc à l'Orange (page 54)*

Ham in Parsley Jelly

Per portion: 8 g fat   250 calories/1050 kJ

1 shin or knuckle of veal, sawn into
pieces
2 calf's feet, coarsely chopped
bouquet garni
4 small onions
8 black peppercorns
600 ml/1 pint dry cider

1 (1.25-kg/2½-lb) piece of ham, all
fat trimmed off
3 tablespoons finely chopped parsley
1 tablespoon wine vinegar
4 tablespoons dry white wine or
cider

Put the first six ingredients into a large pan and bring to the boil, adding enough water to cover the bones. Remove the scum as it rises to the surface. Cover the pan and cook gently for 3 hours, to make a strong stock. Meanwhile, soak the ham in cold water for the same time, to remove some of the saltiness.

Drain the ham and place in the strained veal stock. Bring back to the boil and remove the scum. Cover and simmer until the ham is tender, about 2 hours. This simmering must be very slow or the ham will toughen. Cool the ham in the stock.

Lightly oil a 1.75-litre/3-pint glass bowl and sprinkle with a little of the parsley. Dice the ham coarsely and press gently into the prepared dish. Strain the stock into a clean bowl through a fine sieve; cool. Skim all the fat from the surface of the stock and use a little stock to moisten the ham. Re-strain the remaining stock through a sieve lined with a wet flannel cloth. Cool until syrupy. Stir in the vinegar, the remaining parsley and the white wine or cider. Pour this over the ham chunks and put it in the refrigerator to set. Serve in slices from the dish or turn out on to a serving plate. *Serves 8*

FROM THE TOP: *Pineapple with Black Grapes (page 110); Spinach Soup (page 28); Saltimbocca (page 58) and Ratatouille (page 94)*

Porc à l'Orange

(Illustrated on page 51)

Per portion: 17 g fat 400 calories/1670 kJ

1.25 kg/2½ lb pork fillet
2 tablespoons seasoned flour
1 tablespoon vegetable oil
chopped rosemary
450 ml/¾ pint light chicken stock
juice of 2 oranges

juice of 1 lemon
2 tablespoons orange-flavoured
  liqueur
2 tablespoons demerara sugar
salt and freshly ground black pepper
orange slices to garnish

Cut the pork fillet into small escalopes 2 cm/¾ in thick and toss them in seasoned flour. Heat the oil in a large pan and gently fry the pork with a little chopped rosemary until tender. Transfer to a hot serving dish and keep warm.

Add the chicken stock to the meat juices in the pan, then stir in the fruit juices, liqueur and sugar. Bring to the boil, stirring, then simmer without a lid until reduced by half. Season, strain over the pork and garnish with orange slices. A green salad would go well with this dish. *Serves 6*

Roast Lamb

Per 100 g/4 oz portion (without visible fat): 8 g fat 190 calories/800 kJ

2 tablespoons lemon juice
2 cloves garlic, halved
sprig of rosemary

1 (1.5-kg/3-lb) leg of lamb
salt and freshly ground black pepper
stock or wine

Place the lemon juice, garlic and rosemary in a roasting tin, add the lamb and season it and roast in a moderately hot oven (200 C, 400 F, gas 6) for 30 minutes. Baste. Reduce the oven temperature to moderate (180 C, 350 F, gas 4) and cook for a further 1½ hours, basting from time to time. Transfer the lamb to a hot carving dish.

Carefully pour away all the fat from the roasting tin and make a sauce by adding a little stock or wine to the juices in the pan. Strain and serve. Remember not to eat any of the meat fat. *Serves 6*

Navarin de Mouton

This dish – a complete meal – is not the lowest in fat but it does taste delicious, and as an occasional treat it won't do any harm!

Per portion: 20 g fat   500 calories/2100 kJ

1.25 kg/2½ lb boned shoulder of lamb
1 tablespoon vegetable oil
1 Spanish onion, chopped
1 clove garlic, crushed
3 tablespoons flour
salt and freshly ground black pepper
300 ml/½ pint white wine
300 ml/½ pint light stock

6 baby carrots
6 baby turnips
12 tiny new potatoes
12 button onions
225 g/8 oz shelled peas
225 g/8 oz shelled broad beans
chopped parsley to garnish

Cut the lamb into 4-cm/1½-in cubes and trim away any excess fat. Heat the oil in a large flameproof casserole and use to brown the lamb, onion and garlic. Sprinkle over the flour and seasoning and mix until it is all absorbed. Gradually blend in the wine and stock and bring to the boil. Cover and simmer gently for 1 hour. Allow to become cold and skim off any fat from the surface.

Now add the vegetables to the lamb, peeled or scraped as necessary: carrots, turnips, potatoes, onions, peas and beans. Return to simmering point, cover and cook gently for a further 30 minutes. Serve sprinkled with chopped parsley. *Serves 8*

Lamb Korma

(Illustrated on page 69)

A gift of a small collection of curry spices gave me the push I needed to start experimenting with Indian cookery. Once you have tried it, the tin of blended curry powder goes to the back of the shelf! This dish is mild and scented.

Per portion: 17 g fat   400 calories/1670 kJ

1.5 kg/3 lb boneless lamb, shoulder
   or leg
300 ml/½ pint low-fat natural yogurt
½ teaspoon crushed cardamom
1½ teaspoons ground cumin
½ teaspoon ground turmeric
100 g/4 oz grated coconut
2 tablespoons stock
3 Spanish onions, chopped

2 cloves garlic, crushed
1 teaspoon ground ginger
salt and freshly ground black pepper
½ teaspoon cayenne
1 cinnamon stick
6 cloves
3 tomatoes, quartered
juice of ½ lemon

Trim the meat of any excess fat and cut into 2.5-cm/1-in cubes. Mix the yogurt with the cardamom, cumin and turmeric. Add the lamb and turn the pieces of meat until well coated. Cover and leave in a cool place for 1 hour.

Simmer the coconut in 300 ml/½ pint water for 15 minutes. Strain the coconut and keep the liquor.

Cook the onions and garlic in the stock until soft. Add the cubes of lamb and yogurt and cook, stirring, for about 5 minutes. Mix in the ginger, black pepper, cayenne, cinnamon stick and cloves. Add the tomatoes (peeled first if you prefer) and salt to taste, then stir in the coconut milk. Bring gently back to the boil, cover and simmer for about 1 hour. Remove the lid if the sauce needs to reduce a little. At the end of the cooking time remove the cinnamon stick and cloves. Finally, adjust the seasoning, add the lemon juice and turn into a hot dish. Serve with rice and a selection of side dishes of your choice; tomato and onion, chutney and poppadoms are all suitable.
Serves 8

Moussaka

Per portion: 13 g fat   300 calories/1250 kJ

450 g/1 lb aubergines, sliced
light stock
1 onion, chopped
2 cloves garlic, crushed
$\frac{1}{2}$ teaspoon dried oregano or
  marjoram
2 tablespoons vegetable oil
2 tomatoes, peeled and chopped
675 g/1$\frac{1}{2}$ lb minced lamb or beef

150 ml/$\frac{1}{4}$ pint red wine
bouquet garni
salt and freshly ground black pepper
300 ml/$\frac{1}{2}$ pint Tomato Sauce (page
  97)
300 ml/$\frac{1}{2}$ pint Béchamel Sauce (page
  100)
50 g/2 oz Edam or Gouda cheese,
  grated

Pat the aubergines dry with absorbent kitchen paper. Heat a little stock in a large frying pan and use to cook the aubergine slices on both sides. Drain on absorbent kitchen paper.

Now make the meat sauce. Fry the onion, garlic and oregano or marjoram in the oil until soft. Add the tomatoes, meat and red wine. Stir with a wooden spoon until the grains of meat are separate. Add the bouquet garni and barely simmer, uncovered, for about 15 minutes. Season to taste.

Make up the tomato and béchamel sauces, following the recipe instructions.

Now assemble the moussaka in a large, shallow, greased ovenproof dish. Begin with the meat sauce then layer the tomato sauce, aubergine slices and béchamel sauce. Finally, sprinkle over the grated cheese. Cook in a moderate oven (180 C, 350 F, gas 4) for 45 minutes.

A salad is all you need serve with this satisfying and substantial Greek dish. *Serves 6*

Saltimbocca

(Illustrated on page 52)

Per portion: 9 g fat   280 calories/1170 kJ

8 slices raw smoked lean ham
8 small leaves fresh sage
8 (50-g/2-oz) thin slices veal fillet
flour to coat

1 tablespoon vegetable oil
150 ml/$\frac{1}{4}$ pint Marsala or white wine
twist of lemon peel
salt and freshly ground black pepper

Place a slice of ham and a sage leaf on each slice of veal fillet. Roll up and tie with cotton. Coat the rolls lightly with flour.

Heat the oil in a non-stick frying pan. Put in the veal rolls and cook on all sides until they start to turn golden. Pour off any remaining oil, pour in the Marsala or wine and add the lemon peel. Simmer gently for about 10 minutes, season to taste and serve on a hot dish, with the sauce spooned over. *Serves 4*

Italian Veal Casserole

Per portion: 6 g fat   210 calories/880 kJ

6 slices shin of veal (each 5 cm/2 in thick), or 675 g/1½ lb pie veal
15 g/½ oz butter or margarine
seasoned flour to coat
150 ml/¼ pint dry white wine
1 Spanish onion, finely chopped
675 g/1½ lb tomatoes, peeled and roughly chopped

1 teaspoon chopped lemon thyme
½ teaspoon dried oregano
150 ml/¼ pint light stock
salt and freshly ground black pepper
1 lemon
2 cloves garlic, crushed (optional)
2 tablespoons chopped parsley

Shin of veal is the traditional flavoursome cut used for this dish. If you are using pie veal, trim and cube it.

Heat the butter or margarine in a heavy-bottomed flameproof casserole. Cook the veal, lightly dusted with seasoned flour, until golden. If using shin, stand the veal upright so the marrow does not fall out of the bone. Add the wine, onion, tomatoes, herbs, stock and seasoning. Bring to simmering point, cover and cook gently for 1½–2 hours. Take off the lid after the first hour if the sauce needs reducing.

Grate the rind of the lemon and mix with the garlic and parsley. Sprinkle over the casserole just before serving. Italian risotto rice, coloured with a pinch of saffron, goes well with this marvellous dish. *Serves 6*

Swedish Meatballs

Per portion: 10–15 g fat   275–320 calories/1150–1330 kJ

450 g/1 lb minced beef
1 medium-sized onion
1 clove garlic
$\frac{1}{2}$ teaspoon ground cumin
$\frac{1}{4}$ teaspoon dried thyme
salt and freshly ground black pepper

about 50 g/2 oz flour
1 tablespoon vegetable oil
300 ml/$\frac{1}{2}$ pint strong beef stock
300 ml/$\frac{1}{2}$ pint low-fat natural yogurt
$\frac{1}{2}$ teaspoon cayenne
chopped parsley to garnish

Peel the onion and chop it finely. Peel and crush the clove of garlic.

Mix the beef, which should be very lean, with the chopped onion, crushed garlic, cumin and thyme. Season to taste with salt and freshly ground black pepper. Shape the mixture into fairly small balls, about the size of walnuts, and dust the balls with a little of the flour. Fry the meatballs in the oil until golden brown, then remove them from the pan with a slotted spoon and drain on absorbent kitchen paper.

Stir the remaining flour into the fat left in the pan. Add the beef stock and bring to the boil, stirring constantly. Simmer the sauce until it is smooth and thick, then stir in the yogurt. Return the meatballs to the sauce and add the cayenne, and a little more salt and freshly ground black pepper. Transfer to an ovenproof casserole and cook, covered, in a moderate oven (180 C, 350 F, gas 4) for 30 minutes.

Sprinkle the chopped parsley over the top and serve the meatballs in their sauce, with plain boiled potatoes and a dish of redcurrant jelly. *Serves 4*

Spaghetti alla Marinara

Taught to my husband by a Tuscan sailor. Very good.

Per portion: 6 g fat 500 calories/2100 kJ

350 g/12 oz spaghetti
salt and freshly ground black pepper
2 Spanish onions, chopped
2 tablespoons stock
1 tablespoon finely chopped
rosemary

2 cloves garlic, crushed
2 (397-g/14-oz) cans tomatoes
5 tablespoons tomato purée
$\frac{1}{2}$ teaspoon sugar
450 g/1 lb lean minced beef

Cook the spaghetti for 10 minutes in plenty of fast-boiling salted water. Drain and toss in plenty of black pepper.

Meanwhile, soften the onions in the stock until soft. Add the rosemary and garlic and fry gently for a little longer. Stir in the tomatoes, tomato purée, seasoning and sugar. Simmer, uncovered, for 10–15 minutes. Mix in the beef and stir until all the grains are separate. Bring gently back to the boil and simmer for 3 minutes only. Serve immediately, piled on the spaghetti.

Note The beef must be good quality, freshly minced and very lean. *Serves 4*

Old English Casserole of Beef

Per portion: 10 g fat   225 calories/940 kJ

1 kg/2 lb shin of beef	1 teaspoon dried mixed herbs
flour to coat	450 ml/¾ pint beef stock
4 large carrots	salt and freshly ground black pepper
1 tablespoon vegetable oil	1 tablespoon grated horseradish
24 shallots	2 tablespoons brandy
1 tablespoon mustard powder	

Trim any fat and gristle from the beef and cut the meat into 2-cm/¾-in cubes. Toss in the flour. Roughly chop the carrots.

Heat the oil in a large casserole and brown the meat rapidly on all sides. Take out and set aside. Add the carrots and shallots to the pan and cook for a few minutes over a low heat, stirring with a wooden spoon. When the vegetables are golden, remove and put with the meat. Sprinkle the mustard and herbs on to the remaining oil and pan juices and stir well. Gradually blend in the stock. Return the meat and vegetables to the pan and add seasoning to taste. Heat through and cover tightly.

Cook in a moderate oven (160 C, 325 F, gas 3) for 2–3 hours, until the meat is tender; you may need to reduce the heat still further after the first hour. Just before serving, stir in the horseradish and brandy. *Serves 6*

Roast Beef Fillet

Per portion: 16 g fat   360 calories/1500 kJ

1.25 kg/2½ lb beef fillet
1 tablespoon vegetable oil
150 ml/¼ pint red wine
FOR THE HORSERADISH SAUCE
2 tablespoons grated horseradish

grated rind and juice of ½ lemon
50 g/2 oz walnuts, chopped
150 ml/¼ pint low-fat natural yogurt

Brush the beef fillet with the vegetable oil and place it on a grid in a roasting tin. Roast the fillet in a moderately hot oven (200 C, 400 F, gas 6) allowing 40–50 minutes, or according to taste. After about 20 minutes, pour off the fat from the roasting tin. Heat the red wine and pour it over the meat, then continue cooking, basting from time to time to keep the meat moist.

To make the horseradish sauce, mix together the grated horseradish, grated lemon rind and juice, chopped walnuts and yogurt. Transfer the sauce to a small sauceboat.

When the beef is cooked to your liking, carve it on to a heated serving dish and strain over the juices from the roasting tin. Serve with the horseradish sauce.

Spinach and baked jacket potatoes make an excellent accompaniment to this dish. *Serves 6*

Casserole of Beef with Wine

Per portion: 11 g fat   330 calories/1380 kJ

1 kg/2 lb lean braising steak
1 tablespoon vegetable oil
2 large onions, chopped
2 cloves garlic, crushed
50 g/2 oz lean smoked bacon, diced
2 tablespoons flour

salt and freshly ground black pepper
$\frac{1}{2}$ teaspoon dried oregano
300 ml/$\frac{1}{2}$ pint dry red wine
5 tablespoons tomato purée, diluted
    in a little water

Cut the beef into 4-cm/1$\frac{1}{2}$-in cubes. Heat the oil in a large, thick-bottomed flameproof casserole and fry the onion and garlic until golden. Add the bacon and cook for a few minutes. Stir in the flour and then add the beef, combining all well together. Season lightly and add the remaining ingredients. Cover and bring slowly to the boil.

Transfer to a cool oven (150 C, 300 F, gas 3) for 2 hours, until tender. Reduce the heat after 1 hour if the casserole is cooking faster than a very gentle bubbling. Adjust for seasoning and serve from the casserole. *Serves 6*

Poultry and Game

Chicken is deservedly popular these days because it can be used to make such a range of good dishes: flambéed with red wine and brandy; grilled with a barbecue sauce; in a delicious wine and tarragon sauce; or simply roast, in the very best manner. Rabbit with mustard, and turkey cooked in a way that tastes nothing like Christmas, all add to this selection of very special poultry and game recipes.

Chicken en Cocotte

Per portion: 5 g fat   310 calories/1300 kJ

1 (1.5-kg/3½-lb) chicken, jointed and
  skinned
salt and freshly ground black pepper
1 tablespoon vegetable oil
50 g/2 oz lean smoked ham, diced
4 small onions, chopped
1 clove garlic, crushed
2 tablespoons brandy

6 tomatoes, peeled and chopped
3 carrots, chopped
2 sticks celery, cut into 4-cm/1½-in
  lengths
¼ teaspoon chopped thyme
bay leaf
300 ml/½ pint red wine
chopped parsley to garnish

Season the chicken portions with salt and pepper. Heat the oil in a flameproof casserole or flambé pan and add the diced ham and chicken portions. Cook until golden, turning. Take out the meats and set aside.

Fry the onions and garlic in the pan fat until softened, stirring. Return the chicken and ham to the pan. Pour on the brandy and flambé the meats. Now add the tomatoes, carrots, celery, thyme, bay leaf and red wine. Bring to the boil, cover and simmer for about 30 minutes, until the chicken and vegetables are tender. Remove the bay leaf before serving and sprinkle with chopped parsley. *Serves 4*

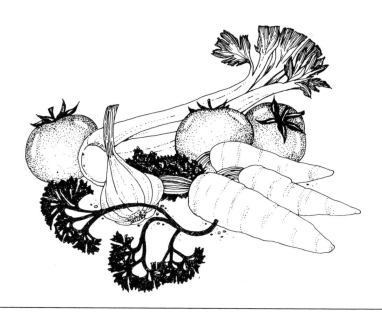

Chicken with White Wine and Tarragon

Per portion: 8 g fat   210 calories/880 kJ

1 (1.5 to 1.75-kg/3½ to 4-lb) chicken, with giblets
salt and freshly ground black pepper
twist of lemon peel
sprig of tarragon
25 g/1 oz butter or margarine

2 tablespoons flour
150 ml/¼ pint dry white wine
2 teaspoons Dijon mustard
2 tablespoons chopped tarragon or ½ teaspoon dried

Sprinkle the chicken with salt and pepper. Tuck the twist of lemon peel and sprig of tarragon inside the chicken. Place in a roasting tin, pour in 300 ml/ ½ pint of water and arrange the giblets round the bird. Cover the tin loosely with foil or greaseproof paper. Cook in a moderately hot oven (200 C, 400 F, gas 6) for 1¼–1½ hours, until cooked. Take up the chicken and joint and carve it. Lay the pieces on a hot dish and cover with the foil or greaseproof paper. Keep warm while you make the sauce.

Melt the butter or margarine in a saucepan. Stir in the flour and cook for 1 minute. Gradually stir in the strained juices from the roasting tin, then add the white wine. Bring to the boil, stirring constantly, and flavour with the mustard and chopped or dried tarragon. Simmer, stirring, for a few minutes. Pour over the chicken and serve immediately. Remember not to eat the chicken skin. *Serves 6*

Stuffed Pot-roasted Chicken

Per portion: 7 g fat   320 calories/1340 kJ

100 g/4 oz long-grain rice
salt and freshly ground black pepper
1 (1.75-kg/4-lb) chicken, with giblets
50 g/2 oz raisins
1 small green pepper, deseeded and
 chopped
grated rind of 1 lemon
450 g/1 lb onions, quartered

450 g/1 lb baby carrots
450 g/1 lb small tomatoes, peeled
 and quartered
$\frac{1}{4}$ teaspoon chopped rosemary
300 ml/$\frac{1}{2}$ pint dry cider
lemon juice
chopped parsley to garnish

Cook the rice in boiling salted water for 10 minutes, until just tender. Drain well. Chop the chicken liver roughly and cook for a few minutes in a little stock. Drain. Mix together the cooked rice, chicken liver, raisins, green pepper, grated lemon rind and seasoning. Stuff the chicken with this mixture.

Grease a casserole dish large enough to take the chicken comfortably. Place the onions, carrots and tomatoes in the bottom and lay the chicken on top. Sprinkle the chicken with the rosemary. Pour the cider round the chicken.

Cover the casserole and cook in a moderate oven (180 C, 350 F, gas 4) for 2 hours, until the chicken is tender. Remove the lid for the last 10 minutes to brown the bird.

Lift out the chicken and place on a hot serving dish. Remove the vegetables carefully with a slotted spoon and arrange round the bird. Strain the juices from the casserole into a small pan and add a squeeze of lemon juice. Reheat and serve separately, in a jug or sauceboat. Garnish the chicken with chopped parsley.

This dish needs only plain boiled potatoes and a crisp green salad. Simply delicious! Remember not to eat the chicken skin. *Serves 6*

FROM THE TOP: *Lemon Sorbet (page 108); Blackcurrant Water Ice (page 109); Lamb Korma (page 56); Rice Pilaf (page 86)*

Roast Chicken with Tarragon

This is the very best way to roast a chicken because it part steams, part roasts, and this preserves the juices and delicious flavour.

Per portion: 7 g fat   200 calories/840 kJ

1 (1.5-kg/3½-lb) roasting chicken,
  with giblets
salt and freshly ground black pepper
chopped tarragon, fresh or dried

twist of lemon peel
cornflour to thicken
white wine or lemon juice

Remove the giblets from the chicken. Sprinkle the inside of the chicken with salt, pepper and a little tarragon, then place the twist of lemon peel inside. Scatter some more tarragon over the outside. Season the bird lightly. Place it in a roasting tin with the giblets and pour in 300 ml/½ pint of hot water. Cover the tin loosely with foil and cook in a moderately hot oven (200 C, 400 F, gas 6) for about 1¼ hours. Check occasionally during cooking that the liquid in the tin has not dried out – add a little more water if it looks low.

When the chicken is ready the leg joints should move freely and when the leg meat is pierced with a fine skewer, the juice that runs should be clear and not pink. Lift the bird on to a hot carving dish, remove the giblets and turn your attention to the beautiful juices left in the pan. Pour off any fat and thicken the juices with a little cornflour moistened in cold water. Then add a dash of white wine or a squeeze of lemon juice, according to taste. Strain and serve. Remember not to eat the chicken skin. *Serves 4*

FROM THE TOP: *Danish Apple Charlotte (page 118); Home-made Yogurt (page 103); Fresh Tomato Soup (page 35); Paprika Chicken (page 72)*

Paprika Chicken

(Illustrated on page 70)

Per portion: 10 g fat   350 calories/1460 kJ

1 (1.5-kg/3-lb) chicken
3 tablespoons chopped fresh
  tarragon or 1 teaspoon dried
300 ml/½ pint giblet stock
FOR THE SAUCE
15 g/½ oz butter or margarine
1 onion, finely chopped
1 clove garlic, crushed
2 teaspoons paprika

2 tablespoons flour
225 g/8 oz tomatoes, peeled and
  chopped
300 ml/½ pint white wine or cider
2 canned pimientos, chopped
salt and freshly ground black pepper
150 ml/¼ pint low-fat natural yogurt
sprig of parsley to garnish

Sprinkle the inside and outside of the chicken with the tarragon. Stand the chicken in a roasting tin, pour round the giblet stock, cover loosely with greaseproof paper or foil and cook in a moderately hot oven (200 C, 400 F, gas 6) for 1¼ hours.

Meanwhile, prepare the sauce. Heat the butter or margarine and use to cook the onion and garlic until quite soft. Sprinkle on the paprika and flour and mix in well. Add the tomatoes, white wine or cider, chopped pimientos and seasoning. Bring to the boil, stirring constantly, and simmer until well reduced. Just before serving, remove from the heat and stir in the yogurt.

Joint or carve the cooked chicken on to a hot dish and pour over the sauce. Serve with pasta, tossed in chopped parsley if you like. Garnish with a sprig of parsley before serving, and remember not to eat the chicken skin.
Serves 4

Hallowe'en Chicken with Sauce Diable

Per portion: 8 g fat   250 calories/1050 kJ

8 chicken portions, skinned
1 tablespoon vegetable oil
salt and black pepper
6 tablespoons Dijon mustard
75 g/3 oz fresh white breadcrumbs,
  dried in the oven
FOR THE SAUCE DIABLE
4 shallots, finely chopped
2 tablespoons black peppercorns,
  crushed

150 ml/¼ pint dry white wine
3 tablespoons wine vinegar
150 ml/¼ pint light stock
2 tablespoons chopped herbs
  (tarragon, chervil and parsley)
2 tablespoons snipped chives
GARNISH
lemon wedges
watercress sprigs

Brush the chicken portions all over with some of the oil. Season with salt and pepper. Cook in a pan under a moderately hot grill for 15 minutes, turning after 8 minutes. Remove from the grill and coat each portion with mustard. Dip in the breadcrumbs, covering well. Replace the chicken under the grill and sprinkle a little more oil on the breadcrumbs as they start to brown. Cook, turning, until golden brown – about 35 minutes.

To make the sauce, boil the shallots, peppercorns, wine and vinegar for about 5 minutes, until reduced by about half. Add the stock and boil for a further 4 minutes. Add the herbs, reheat and pour into a hot sauceboat.

Place the chicken portions in a serving basket. Arrange the lemon wedges and watercress sprigs over the chicken. Hand the sauce separately and serve with baked jacket potatoes. *Serves 8*

Grilled Devilled Chicken

Per portion: 7 g fat   200 calories/840 kJ

1 (1.5-kg/3½-lb) chicken, jointed and skinned, or 4 chicken portions, skinned
1 tablespoon French mustard
1 teaspoon ground ginger
1 teaspoon salt

1 teaspoon freshly ground black pepper
1 teaspoon Worcestershire sauce
½ teaspoon sugar
juice of 1 lemon

Place the chicken portions in a shallow ovenproof dish. Mix together the mustard, ginger, salt, pepper, Worcestershire sauce, sugar and lemon juice. Use to coat the chicken portions and leave to marinate for several hours, turning occasionally in the marinade.

Place the chicken portions under a preheated grill, not too close. Allow 15–20 minutes on each side, although cooking time may be shorter if you do this on an outside barbecue.

Serve with a green salad and Rice Pilaf (page 86). *Serves 4*

Andalusian Chicken

(Illustrated on page 87)

Per portion: 7 g fat 350 calories/1460 kJ

1 (2-kg/4½-lb) roasting chicken
salt and freshly ground black pepper
1 teaspoon dried mixed herbs
225 g/8 oz Spanish onions, chopped
450 g/1 lb green peppers, deseeded
  and diced
4 tomatoes, peeled, deseeded and
  roughly chopped
2 cloves garlic, crushed

1 tablespoon vegetable oil
225 g/8 oz peas, cooked
350 g/12 oz long-grain rice
pinch of saffron powder
bay leaf
GARNISH
2 unpeeled prawns (optional)
lemon slices
chopped parsley

Sprinkle the chicken with salt, pepper and the herbs and stand it in a roasting tin. Pour a cup of water round the chicken. Cover loosely with greased greaseproof paper or foil and roast in a moderately hot oven (200 C, 400 F, gas 6) for 1½ hours. Cool the chicken slightly, discard the skin, then strip the flesh from the bones and cut it into bite-sized pieces. Set aside. Use the chicken carcass and giblets to make chicken stock to cook the rice.

Gently fry the onions, peppers, tomatoes and garlic in the oil until soft and golden. Stir in the cooked drained peas.

Cook the rice in 900 ml/1½ pints chicken stock, with the saffron and bay leaf, for about 10 minutes, until tender. Drain if necessary (the rice should be quite dry) and remove the bay leaf.

Now fold the chicken and rice into the onion mixture. Pile into a large, heated serving dish and garnish with the prawns, if using, and lemon slices. Serve, sprinkled with parsley. *Serves 8*

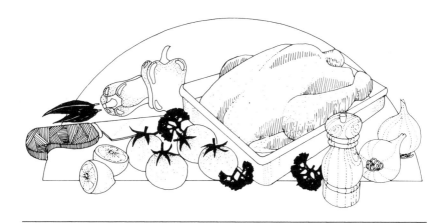

Cold Lemon Chicken

This makes a lovely buffet dish and provides leftover stock and vegetables to use for soup the following day.

Per portion: 8 g fat   250 calories/1050 kJ

1 (1.75-kg/4-lb) chicken
1 onion, peeled and sliced
225 g/8 oz carrots, peeled and cut
  into julienne strips
1 lemon
salt and white pepper
2 egg yolks

1 tablespoon cornflour
300 ml/½ pint low-fat natural yogurt
450 g/1 lb fresh or 225 g/8 oz frozen
  asparagus, cooked and cooled
GARNISH
lemon wedges
watercress sprigs

Place the chicken in a large saucepan with the giblets, onion and carrot. Cover with water, add 2 twists of lemon peel and seasoning, then cover the pan and simmer for 45–55 minutes, until tender. Cool the chicken and remove the flesh from the bones. Cut the meat into bite-sized pieces, discarding any skin.

Blend about 300 ml/½ pint of the strained stock with the juice of the lemon, the egg yolks and cornflour. Cook this carefully in a double boiler until the sauce is smooth and coats the back of the wooden spoon. Cool and beat in the yogurt. Thin with a little more chicken stock if necessary and adjust seasoning.

Lay the chicken on a serving dish and mask with the lemon sauce. Arrange the cooked asparagus on top in a lattice pattern, put three wedges of lemon at each corner and garnish with watercress sprigs. Accompany with a tossed green salad or a selection of salads. *Serves 6*

Chicken, Celery and Walnut Salad

Per portion: 8 g fat 175 calories/730 kJ

1 (2-kg/4½-lb) chicken, with giblets
3 sprigs tarragon
1 large head celery, chopped
50 g/2 oz walnuts, coarsely chopped
2 tablespoons chopped parsley

300 ml/½ pint oil-free French
  dressing
salt and freshly ground black pepper
GARNISH
watercress sprigs
lettuce hearts

Remove the giblets and sprinkle the chicken with the chopped tarragon leaves. Place in a roasting tin and surround with the giblets. Pour in 300 ml/½ pint of water. Cover the tin loosely with greaseproof paper or foil and cook in a moderately hot oven (200 C, 400 F, gas 6) for 1–1¼ hours. Allow to cool.

Discard the chicken skin. Remove all the chicken meat from the bones and cut it into bite-sized pieces. Combine with the celery, walnuts and parsley. Toss in enough French dressing to moisten and season to taste.

Pile on to a serving dish and surround with small bunches of watercress and lettuce hearts. *Serves 8*

Traditional Roast Turkey

**Per portion (100 g/4 oz meat $+\frac{1}{8}$ of stuffing and gravy):   5 g fat
350 calories/1460 kJ**

1 (4.5-kg/10-lb) turkey
1 tablespoon dried basil
salt and freshly ground black pepper
600 ml/1 pint good stock
5 tablespoons port
1 tablespoon cornflour
FOR THE STUFFINGS
450 g/1 lb chestnuts
175 g/6 oz mashed potato

salt and freshly ground black pepper
65 g/2½ oz fresh breadcrumbs
1 heaped tablespoon sultanas
1 clove garlic, crushed
2 sticks celery, finely chopped
2 tablespoons chopped parsley
grated rind of 1 lemon
a little grated fresh root ginger
3 tablespoons medium-dry sherry

Prepare the stuffings for the neck and carcass in advance. Make a slit on the rounded side of the chestnuts. Drop, four at a time, into small pans of boiling water for 3 minutes. Peel and skin. Cook the peeled chestnuts gently in fresh boiling water for about 20 minutes. Drain, then mash with a fork. Mix a quarter of the chestnuts with the mashed potato and seasoning. Use to stuff the neck of the bird. Mix the remaining chestnuts with the rest of the stuffing ingredients and use to stuff the turkey carcass.

Stand the bird in a large roasting tin and sprinkle with basil and seasoning. Pour the stock round the bird and cover the tin loosely with a piece of greased foil. Cook in a moderate oven (180 C, 350 F, gas 4), allowing 15–20 minutes per 500 g/1 lb, plus 20 minutes extra. Turn the turkey, on its side or upright, every 30 minutes, and baste frequently with the pan juices.

Remove the foil 20 minutes before the end of the cooking time, to brown the bird, turning it breast side up. Pour off the pan juices to make gravy. Skim off all the fat and boil up the juices with the port. Moisten the cornflour with a little cold water and stir into the gravy, to thicken. Keep warm in a sauceboat until ready to serve. Remember not to eat the turkey skin.

Turkey in Vermouth

Per portion: (100 g/4 oz meat + ⅙ of stuffing): 5 g fat 250 calories/1000 kJ

1 (3.25 to 3.5-kg/7 to 8-lb) turkey
1 tablespoon chopped tarragon
1 small onion, chopped
2 sticks celery, chopped
4 medium-sized carrots, chopped
300 ml/½ pint dry white vermouth
FOR THE STUFFING
75 g/3 oz fresh white breadcrumbs

grated rind of 1½ lemons
4 tablespoons chopped parsley
½ teaspoon chopped thyme
salt and freshly ground black pepper
100 g/4 oz green grapes, halved and
  pipped
1 egg, beaten

Mix together the dry stuffing ingredients and bind with just enough egg. Do not make the mixture too wet. Spoon the stuffing into the bird. Sprinkle the turkey with the chopped tarragon. Lay the onion, celery and carrots in the base of a large oblong casserole dish or roasting tin. Place the turkey on the bed of vegetables and pour round the vermouth. Cover and cook in a moderately hot oven (190 C, 375 F, gas 5) for 2½–3 hours, or until cooked. Baste from time to time with the pan juices. Add a little hot giblet stock or water, if necessary, to keep the dish moist.

The turkey will be succulent and tender. Slice the flesh and serve with a spoonful of stuffing and the strained juices from the casserole. Remember not to eat the turkey skin. *Serves 6*

Faisan en Casserole

Per portion (100 g/4 oz meat + $\frac{1}{6}$ of sauce and bread):   15 g fat
400 calories/1670 kJ

a brace of pheasants
1 tablespoon vegetable oil
2 onions, chopped
2 tablespoons flour
600 ml/1 pint good stock
2 teaspoons redcurrant jelly
rind and juice of 1 orange

150 ml/$\frac{1}{4}$ pint port or red wine
bouquet garni
salt and freshly ground black pepper
4 slices bread, crusts removed
25 g/1 oz butter or margarine
chopped parsley to garnish

Brown the pheasants gently in a flameproof casserole with the oil, turning and making sure they don't catch. Transfer to a plate and keep warm.

Fry the onions gently in the remaining fat until softened. Sprinkle over the flour and stir until blended. Gradually add the stock, stirring, then the redcurrant jelly, grated orange rind and juice, port or red wine, bouquet garni and seasoning. Simmer, stirring, for 1 minute. Return the pheasants to the pan and spoon the sauce over them.

Cover and cook slowly on top of the cooker, or in a moderate oven (160 C, 325 F, gas 3), for 1 hour, or until the meat is tender. Remove the pheasants and carve and joint them; cover and keep warm. Reserve the sauce.

Cut the bread slices with a small heart-shaped cutter, spread with butter or margarine and grill to brown. Keep warm. When ready to serve, arrange the pheasant pieces on a large heated serving dish, spoon a little sauce over and dredge parsley down the centre. Surround with the heart-shaped croûtons. Heat through the rest of the sauce and hand separately. Remove the skin before eating. *Serves 6*

Civet de Lièvre

**Per portion (100 g/4 oz meat + $\frac{1}{8}$ of remaining ingredients): 12 g fat
450 calories/1880 kJ**

1 hare, jointed
1 tablespoon vegetable oil
100 g/4 oz smoked bacon, trimmed
  of fat and diced
12 button onions
2 tablespoons flour
24 chestnuts, peeled (see Traditional
  Roast Turkey, page 78)
2 teaspoons redcurrant jelly

FOR THE MARINADE
1 onion, chopped
1 carrot, chopped
15 g/$\frac{1}{2}$ oz butter or margarine
$\frac{3}{4}$–1 bottle red wine
salt and freshly ground black pepper
bouquet garni
2 cloves garlic, crushed

The hare should be adequately hung and carefully jointed by your butcher. It will need to be marinated for a day or two, so plan well ahead.

To prepare the marinade, cook the onion and carrot for a few minutes in the butter or margarine, then add the remaining marinade ingredients. Pour over the hare portions in a deep flameproof casserole. Cover. Marinate for 1–2 days, turning the meat occasionally.

When you are ready to cook the dish, remove the hare portions and lay on a plate. Keep the marinade in a bowl by the cooker. Rinse and dry the casserole.

Heat the oil in the casserole and use to brown the bacon and button onions. Take out the onions and reserve. Sprinkle the flour over the bacon and stir. Put in the hare portions, pour over the marinade, stirring to incorporate, and bring gently to the boil. Barely simmer, covered, for 1$\frac{1}{2}$–2 hours. Thirty minutes before the end of the cooking time, add the button onions, chestnuts and redcurrant jelly.

Remove the hare portions, the button onions and the chestnuts and place on a large hot serving dish. Reduce the sauce if necessary (boil rapidly, stirring, without a lid) and then strain over the meat.

Hand extra redcurrant jelly separately and serve with puréed potatoes and a fresh green vegetable. *Serves 8*

Polly's Lapin à la Moutarde

This is a recipe from a friend on the island of Ibiza.

Per portion (100 g/4 oz meat+$\frac{1}{4}$ of sauce):   12 g fat   350 calories/1460 kJ

3 tablespoons Dijon mustard
2 tablespoons fresh breadcrumbs
1 tablespoon vegetable oil
1 oven-ready young rabbit

1 heaped tablespoon cornflour
300 ml/$\frac{1}{2}$ pint white wine or cider
salt and freshly ground black pepper
2 tablespoons low-fat natural yogurt

Mix together the mustard, breadcrumbs and oil. Coat the rabbit with this mixture, place in a roasting tin and cook in a moderately hot oven (200 C, 400 F, gas 6) for 50 minutes, or until tender. Lift the rabbit on to a hot carving dish and keep warm.

Mix the cornflour with a little cold water and pour into the roasting tin with the wine or cider. Cook gently on top of the cooker for a few minutes, stirring with a wooden spoon. Season, remove from the heat and stir in the yogurt. Strain into a warm sauceboat and serve with the rabbit. *Serves 4*

Vegetable Dishes and Salads

As some of the more exotic vegetables become widely available, so has vegetable cooking become more imaginative and unusual; try a casserole of aubergines with cottage cheese, Jerusalem artichokes with tomatoes and garlic, or that constant French favourite, ratatouille. Salads are no longer simply summer fare; many winter vegetables are delicious used raw to make crisp, crunchy salads, especially with the addition of some chopped nuts or fruit, all tossed in a piquant dressing.

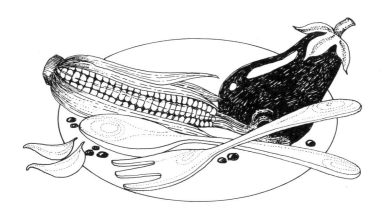

Braised Fennel

*Celery can be treated in the same way. Serve as a first course, or as a
vegetable with fish and meat dishes.*

Per portion: 0 g fat   20 calories/85 kJ

2 bulbs fennel
salt

300 ml/½ pint stock

Trim and rinse the fennel. Cut each bulb in half and blanch in boiling salted
water for 5 minutes. Drain thoroughly.

Place the fennel in a shallow ovenproof dish and pour over the stock.
Cover the dish with a lid or foil and cook in a moderately hot oven (190 C,
375 F, gas 5) for 20–30 minutes, until tender. *Serves 4*

Red Cabbage

Good with winter and Christmas dishes.

Per portion: 0 g fat   100 calories/420 kJ

1 kg/2 lb red cabbage
5 tablespoons red wine vinegar
1 onion, chopped
2 crisp green apples, peeled and
  chopped

1 teaspoon caraway seeds
1 teaspoon salt
freshly ground black pepper
2 tablespoons demerera sugar

Cut the cabbage in half lengthways and remove the thick white stalk. Shred
the cabbage finely.

Put the vinegar in a large, heavy-based pan. Add 5 tablespoons of water,
the cabbage, onion, apples and remaining ingredients. Stir well, bring to
boiling point then cover and cook gently for 50 minutes–1 hour, stirring
from time to time, until the cabbage is tender. Add more water if necessary
during the cooking to prevent the cabbage boiling dry. *Serves 6*

Courgettes

Per portion: 3 g fat   50 calories/210 kJ

675 g/1½ lb courgettes, sliced
15 g/½ oz butter or margarine
stock
1 clove garlic, crushed

juice of ½ lemon
freshly ground black pepper
sea salt
chopped parsley to garnish

Fry the courgettes in the butter or margarine and a little stock, with the garlic, lemon juice and pepper, until they are soft and golden brown; turn once during cooking. Season with salt, sprinkle over parsley and serve.

Add some peeled, deseeded and roughly chopped tomatoes to the courgettes to make Courgettes Provençale. *Serves 4*

Aubergine Casserole

Per portion: 0 g fat   60 calories/250 kJ

3–4 medium-sized aubergines, sliced
salt and freshly ground black pepper
stock
225 g/8 oz cottage cheese

8 tomatoes, peeled and sliced
4 tablespoons fresh breadcrumbs
1 clove garlic, crushed

Sprinkle the aubergine slices liberally with salt and leave to drain in a colander for about 1 hour. This removes any bitterness. Rinse and pat dry, then cook in stock until tender. Drain on absorbent kitchen paper.

Lightly oil a deep ovenproof dish, place a layer of aubergine slices in the bottom, season and cover with cottage cheese. Season again and cover with a layer of tomato slices. Repeat the layers until the ingredients are used up, then top with the breadcrumbs and garlic. Cook in a moderately hot oven (190 C, 375 F, gas 5) for 40–45 minutes. *Serves 6*

Rice Pilaf

(Illustrated on page 69)

Per portion: 0 g fat 250 calories/1050 kJ

225 g/8 oz long-grain rice
salt
1 onion, chopped
stock

1 teaspoon ground turmeric
1 tablespoon currants
1 (226-g/8-oz) can pineapple pieces, drained

Cook the rice in boiling salted water for 10 minutes. Drain and sprinkle with a little cold water to separate the grains. Keep warm in a covered dish.

Cook the onion in a little stock and add the turmeric, currants and pineapple pieces. Drain. Toss the rice in this mixture and serve. *Serves 4*

Riced Potatoes

Plain boiled potatoes are made into a lovely light snow by an old-fashioned gadget, obtainable from most caterers' suppliers and some kitchen shops, called simply a potato ricer.

Use the ricer for cooked swedes as well. Mix the riced swedes with a little crushed garlic, and season well with sea salt and freshly ground black pepper. Not a bit like school veg!

FROM THE TOP: *Gazpacho (page 36), with accompaniments at the bottom; Andalusian Chicken (page 75); Gooseberry Fool (page 112)*

French Beans and Mushrooms Vinaigrette

Per portion: 0 g fat   40 calories/175 kJ

1 kg/2 lb frozen whole French beans
salt
450 g/1 lb button mushrooms
juice of ½ lemon
½ small onion, grated

a little ground coriander
3 tablespoons chopped parsley
250 ml/scant ½ pint oil-free French
  dressing

Cook the beans in boiling salted water until just tender, then cool under running water. Drain thoroughly.

Wipe the mushrooms with a clean damp cloth and slice finely. Sprinkle with lemon juice. Add the onion, coriander and parsley to the French dressing, then pour over the mushrooms. Turn gently for an hour or two.

Toss the mushroom mixture carefully with the French beans and serve in a simple china dish. *Serves 8*

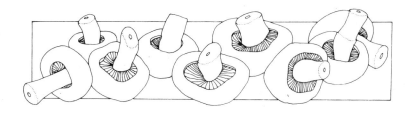

FROM THE TOP: *Fruit Cake (page 120); Brandy Snaps (page 123); Angel Cake (page 124)*

Topinambours Provençale

Per portion: 0 g fat   50 calories/210 kJ

1 kg/2 lb Jerusalem artichokes,
   scraped
2 large cloves garlic, crushed
450 g/1 lb tomatoes, peeled, deseeded
   and chopped
2 tablespoons tomato purée

juice of ½ lemon
1 tablespoon chopped basil or
   ½ teaspoon dried
1 teaspoon sugar
salt and freshly ground black pepper
2 tablespoons chopped parsley

Slice the artichokes thickly and steam or poach them until tender, about 20 minutes.

Meanwhile, mix the garlic and the tomatoes and cook for about 10 minutes, stirring frequently, until the liquid has reduced a little. When the texture is pulpy, add the tomato purée, lemon juice, basil, sugar and seasoning. Heat through and pour over the cooked artichokes in a serving dish. Just before serving sprinkle with chopped parsley. This dish is equally delicious served hot or cold. *Serves 6*

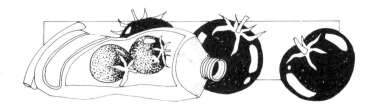

Spaghetti with Mushrooms

Per portion: 10 g fat   400 calories/1670 kJ

450 g/1 lb spaghetti
sea salt and freshly ground black
  pepper
225 g/8 oz button mushrooms, wiped
  and sliced
25 g/1 oz butter or margarine

1 tablespoon flour
150 ml/$\frac{1}{4}$ pint dry white wine
300 ml/$\frac{1}{2}$ pint low-fat natural yogurt
3 egg yolks
3 tablespoons chopped chives, or to
  taste

Boil the spaghetti fast in a large pan of salted water for approximately 10 minutes. Drain and season to taste.

Meanwhile, sauté the mushrooms in the butter or margarine. Sprinkle on the flour, stir in the wine and cook for a few minutes. Blend the yogurt with the egg yolks, chives and seasoning. Add carefully to the pan. Heat through, stirring with a wooden spoon, without allowing the egg yolks to curdle. Serve immediately, tossed into or poured over the pasta. Sprinkle with extra chopped chives, if liked. *Serves 6*

Carrot Salad

Per portion: 0 g fat   80 calories/330kJ

450 g/1 lb carrots, grated
juice of 2 oranges

2 tablespoons raisins
salt and freshly ground black pepper

Simply toss all together. *Serves 4*

Rice Salad

Per portion: 1 g fat   250 calories/1050 kJ

450 g/1 lb long-grain rice
salt
1 (184-g/6½-oz) can pimientos,
  rinsed and chopped
1 (340-g/12-oz) can sweet corn,
  drained

1 teaspoon chopped lemon thyme
2 tablespoons chopped parsley
250 ml/scant ½ pint oil-free French
  dressing

Cook the rice in boiling salted water for 10 minutes. Drain and sprinkle with cold water to separate the grains. Combine with the remaining ingredients and pour over enough French dressing to moisten. Toss well together and cool.

Peach and Ginger Salad

This is a good starter, and an excellent accompaniment to cold meats.

Per portion: 0 g fat   120 calories/500 kJ

3 peaches
juice of ½ lemon
4 pieces preserved ginger, sliced
1 lettuce heart

3 tablespoons oil-free French
  dressing
chopped parsley to garnish

Scald the peaches by plunging them into a bowl of boiling water for 1 minute. Skin and slice and sprinkle with lemon juice. Mix with the sliced ginger and arrange on a bed of lettuce. Spoon over the French dressing and scatter with parsley. *Serves 4*

Coleslaw

Per portion: 0 g fat   90 calories/375 kJ

1 small white cabbage
4 Cox's apples
juice of 1 lemon
1 head celery
50 g/2 oz walnuts, chopped
2 tablespoons chopped parsley

2 tablespoons snipped chives
1 green pepper, deseeded and
  chopped
250 ml/scant ½ pint oil-free French
  dressing

Shred the cabbage finely, discarding the tough white stalk. Core and chop the apples (leaving the skin on) and toss in the lemon juice. Wash and chop the celery, using the tender inside leaves and stalks. Place the cabbage, apples, celery and remaining ingredients in a large bowl. Pour over enough French dressing to coat and toss all together well. *Serves 8*

Obbie's Salad

Per portion: 8 g fat   140 calories/580 kJ

50 g/2 oz halved blanched almonds
½ small white cabbage, finely
  shredded
225 g/8 oz grated carrot, marinated
  in fresh orange juice
1 lettuce, shredded

2 pork sausages, well grilled and
  sliced
3 peaches
150 ml/¼ pint oil-free French
  dressing

Grill the almonds.
    Assemble the cabbage, carrot, lettuce and sausage slices in a large bowl. Just before serving, peel and slice the peaches and add to the salad with the French dressing and almonds. Toss all together and serve. *Serves 6*

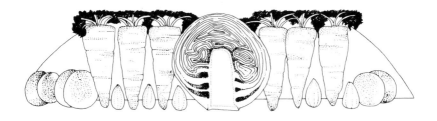

Ratatouille

(Illustrated on page 52)

This can also be served as a starter, either hot or cold depending on the rest of the meal and the state of the weather. Assemble the ingredients, prepare them in the order given, and the cooking times will be just right. You will need a large, heavy-based sauté pan with a lid.

Per portion: 0 g fat   60 calories/250 kJ

2 aubergines, cubed
salt and freshly ground black pepper
2 large Spanish onions, sliced
150 ml/¼ pint stock
2 cloves garlic, crushed
3 green peppers, deseeded and diced
4 courgettes, sliced

8 ripe tomatoes, peeled and chopped
½ teaspoon dried thyme
1 teaspoon dried oregano
1 teaspoon sugar
chopped parsley or black olives to
    garnish (optional)

Place the aubergines in a colander, sprinkle with salt and leave to drain for 30 minutes. Rinse and pat dry.

Soften the onions in the stock and then add the vegetables as you prepare them, turning well with each addition. Add the aubergines at the same time as the courgettes. Toss in the herbs, seasoning and sugar, cover and cook gently for a further 20–30 minutes, stirring from time to time. Drain at the end of cooking time if necessary.

Serve hot, sprinkled with chopped parsley if liked, or cold on a bed of lettuce leaves, garnished with black olives. *Serves 6*

Sauces and Basic Recipes

All together in one useful section are those recipes that form every cook's standby, and which are referred to constantly; the basic sauces, and some sauces for special occasions, recipes for home-made yogurt, curd cheese and salad dressing, plus a basic pancake batter – always useful to make a quick and tasty supper dish, served with a savoury filling or sweet sauce.

Cumberland Sauce

To serve with Christmas ham, game and cold meats, or to make as a gift.

Total recipe: 0 g fat   1000 calories/4200 kJ

1 small onion, finely chopped
2 oranges
1 lemon
1 (227-g/8-oz) jar redcurrant jelly

1 teaspoon Dijon mustard
150 ml/¼ pint port
2 teaspoons cornflour

Put the chopped onion in a small saucepan. Pare the rind of 1 orange and the lemon with a potato peeler, cut the rind into very thin strips and add to the onion. Cover with cold water, bring to the boil and cook for 5 minutes. Drain.

Put the redcurrant jelly in a heatproof bowl over a saucepan of boiling water. Stir the jelly until melted. Push through a sieve to remove any lumps, if necessary, then return to the bowl over simmering water. Stir in the mustard, port, the juice of both oranges and the lemon, and the blanched rind and onion. Cook for 5 minutes then stir in the cornflour moistened with 1 tablespoon cold water. Simmer for a further 2–3 minutes, stirring, then pour into a jar and leave to cool.

Seal tightly and leave for a week before using. This sauce will keep for about two months but it should be stored in the refrigerator once opened.
Serves 8

Anchovy Sauce

Lovely as a dip with crudités.

Total recipe: 1 g fat   170 calories/710 kJ

1 (56-g/2-oz) can anchovy fillets,
    soaked in milk
150 g/5 oz cottage cheese

2 teaspoons lemon juice
5 drops Tabasco sauce (optional)
3 tablespoons low-fat natural yogurt

Liquidise the ingredients in a blender or food processor, or work them together with a wooden spoon in the order listed, until you have obtained a smooth sauce. *Makes about 250 ml/8 fl oz*

Velouté Sauce

Total recipe: 21 g fat   375 calories/1570 kJ

25 g/1 oz butter or margarine
40 g/1½ oz flour

600 ml/1 pint chicken or veal stock
salt and white pepper

Melt the butter or margarine and stir in the flour to form a roux. Heat the stock to boiling and add to the roux a little at a time, stirring vigorously with a wooden spoon or whisk. Cook the sauce for at least 6–7 minutes, stirring constantly; the sauce should be the thickness of runny cream. Season to taste and strain through a sieve before serving.
Note Fish velouté is made in exactly the same way, using fish stock. *Makes 600 ml/1 pint*

Tomato Sauce

Total recipe: 0 g fat   240 calories/1000 kJ

1 Spanish onion, chopped
2 tablespoons stock
1 clove garlic, crushed
½ teaspoon dried oregano
2 (397-g/14-oz) cans tomatoes
5 tablespoons tomato purée

1 teaspoon sugar
1 teaspoon salt
freshly ground black pepper
bay leaf
twist of lemon rind

Soften the onion in the stock. Add the remaining ingredients and bring to the boil, stirring. Cover and simmer for 15 minutes. Remove the lemon rind and bay leaf and adjust the seasoning. *Makes about 600 ml/1 pint*

Cranberry Sauce

Total recipe: 0 g fat   320 calories/1340 kJ

175 g/6 oz cranberries
150 ml/¼ pint water
2 tablespoons demerara sugar

a little grated orange rind
2 tablespoons brandy

Place all the ingredients in a saucepan. Cook over gentle heat, stirring, until the cranberries pop and burst. Serve hot, in a sauceboat, to accompany roast turkey. *Serves 6*

Cucumber and Mint Sauce

Total recipe: 3 g fat   190 calories/790 kJ

½ cucumber, thinly sliced
1½ teaspoons salt
300 ml/½ pint low-fat natural yogurt

2 tablespoons chopped mint
salt and pepper

Sprinkle the cucumber with the salt and leave to drain for an hour in a colander. Press gently to drain off any surplus juice. Turn the cucumber into a bowl and stir in the yogurt and chopped mint. Season to taste with salt and pepper. *Makes 450 ml/¾ pint.*

Cucumber Sauce

Excellent with mackerel or cold salmon.

Total recipe: 0 g fat   180 calories/750 kJ

½ cucumber, peeled, deseeded and
  chopped
salt and white pepper

225 g/8 oz cottage cheese, sieved
2 tablespoons low-fat natural yogurt
2 tablespoons chopped mint

Sprinkle the cucumber lightly with salt and drain in a colander for 15 minutes. Blend the cucumber and cottage cheese in the liquidiser with enough yogurt to bring the sauce to the consistency of thick cream. Stir in the mint and season to taste. *Makes 150 ml/¼ pint*

Mustard Sauce

This sauce is excellent with all sausage, pork and ham dishes and as an accompaniment to crudités. It is also a good sauce to serve with mackerel and herring.

Total recipe: 25 g fat   300 calories/1250 kJ

2 tablespoons Dijon mustard
150 ml/¼ pint low-fat natural yogurt

150 ml/¼ pint Soft Curd Cheese (page
  104)
1 teaspoon vinegar

Whizz the ingredients in your blender or food processor, or beat together with a rotary whisk in a bowl. Turn out into a small bowl. *Makes about 300 ml/½ pint*

Béchamel Sauce

Total recipe: 21 g fat   575 calories/2400 kJ

25 g/1 oz butter or margarine
40 g/1½ oz flour
600 ml/1 pint skimmed milk

salt and white pepper
bay leaf (optional)

Melt the butter or margarine in a saucepan and blend in the flour. Cook for 1 minute. Add a little of the milk and when it bubbles, beat with a wooden spoon until smooth. Continue adding the rest of the milk like this. Season to taste and cook gently for at least 5 minutes, stirring constantly. Infuse the bay leaf in this, if liked, to give a stronger flavour to the sauce. *Makes 600 ml/1 pint*

Garlic Sauce

Serve this sauce as a dunk for raw vegetables.

Total recipe: 6 g fat   230 calories/960 kJ

2 cloves garlic, crushed
150 g/5 oz Soft Curd Cheese (page 104)
1 teaspoon dried mixed herbs

2 teaspoons lemon juice
3 tablespoons low-fat natural yogurt
½ teaspoon celery salt

Liquidise the ingredients in the blender or food processor, or work them together with a wooden spoon in a mixing bowl. Serve from a small bowl. *Makes about 225 ml/7½ fl oz*

Mushroom Sauce

This is a good accompaniment for fish, chicken and veal dishes.

Total recipe: 24 g fat   680 calories/2850 kJ

1 small onion, peeled and chopped
25 g/1 oz butter or margarine
225 g/8 oz button mushrooms, wiped and sliced
juice of ½ lemon
2 tablespoons flour

300 ml/½ pint dry cider or white wine
½ teaspoon Worcestershire sauce
salt and pepper
300 ml/½ pint low-fat natural yogurt

Soften the onion in the butter or margarine and add the mushrooms and lemon juice. Shake over the flour and stir in for a minute or two. Gradually add the cider or wine, stirring all the time, and bring to the boil. Season with Worcestershire sauce, salt and pepper. Simmer for a few minutes and stir in the yogurt just before serving. *Makes about 600 ml/1 pint*

Low-fat Soured Cream

Total recipe: 0 g fat   140 calories/580 kJ

2 tablespoons skimmed milk
1 tablespoon lemon juice

225 g/8 oz cottage cheese
¼ teaspoon salt

Measure the ingredients into a liquidiser in the order listed above. Cover and blend for 30 seconds or until smooth. Chill.

Snipped chives are excellent stirred into this, to accompany meat or fish or to top a baked jacket potato. Or serve as a dressing for salad, or as a sauce for a mousse with the addition of some freshly chopped tarragon or dill. If using in a hot dish, add at the last moment. *Makes 150 ml/¼ pint*

Pancake Batter

Per pancake: 1 g fat 90 calories/375 kJ

100 g/4 oz plain flour
½ teaspoon salt
2 teaspoons caster sugar (for sweet
  batters only)

1 egg
about 300 ml/½ pint skimmed milk
vegetable oil for frying

Sift the flour, salt and sugar into a large bowl. Mix the egg and milk and add slowly to the dry ingredients. Beat well and then set aside for 1 hour. The batter should be like runny cream; add more milk if necessary.

Place a medium-sized non-stick frying pan on top of the cooker and heat gently. Rub the base of the hot pan with absorbent kitchen paper dipped in oil, and pour in just enough batter to coat the bottom. When tiny bubbles appear in the pancake, lift up the edges and peep underneath; if it is golden toss the pancake in the air to turn and cook the other side.

The pancakes can be stacked and kept warm, or reheated over a pan of boiling water. Re-oil the pan between each pancake. *Makes about 8*

Home-made Yogurt

(Illustrated on page 70)

Total recipe: 6 g fat   270 calories/1130 kJ

150 ml/5 fl oz unsweetened low-fat
natural yogurt

600 ml/1 pint skimmed milk, made
up using 100 g/4 oz skimmed milk
powder

Mix together the yogurt and skimmed milk in a bowl, cover and leave in a
warm place, such as the airing cupboard, for 4–6 hours, or until set
(depending on the warmth). Stir once, then chill in the refrigerator before
use. Save some at the end to make up the next batch of yogurt.

It is marvellous for breakfast with fresh fruit and muesli, will add to soups
and sauces, makes a delicious sweet with puréed or whole fruits and can be
eaten on its own with a spoonful of honey or soft brown sugar. It is so
convenient to always keep a bowl of yogurt in the refrigerator; I wish I could
sell it to you strongly enough! *Makes 750 ml/1¼ pints*

Yogurt Dressing

This is a delicious, easily made and unusual dressing to serve with salads.

Total recipe: 2 g fat   90 calories/375 kJ

150 ml/¼ pint low-fat natural yogurt
1 tablespoon tomato ketchup
½ teaspoon paprika
2 tablespoons chopped fresh chives

sea salt and freshly ground black
pepper
2 teaspoons vinegar

Combine the ingredients in the order listed and taste for the exact effect you
want, adjusting quantities to suit. Always taste as you go in cooking. *Makes
just over 150 ml/¼ pint*

Soft Curd Cheese

Total recipe: 3 g fat   900 calories/3770 kJ

2.25 litres/4 pints skimmed milk   1 tablespoon rennet
300 ml/$\frac{1}{2}$ pint low-fat natural yogurt

Sterilise all equipment before beginning.

Heat the milk to blood heat and add the yogurt and rennet. Pour into a clear bowl, cover and leave in a warm place to set (8–10 hours). Strain off the whey, put the curd into a muslin or fine cotton bag and strain again (a colander or sieve is ideal for this purpose). Leave for 1 hour and then replace with fresh muslin. Allow to drip again until the dripping stops (approximately 2 hours). Replace with fresh muslin and chill in the refrigerator before using.

This cheese can be used in cooking or eaten just as it is; it is very useful to thicken a sauce that might otherwise call for egg yolks or cream; it can be substituted for cream cheese in recipes; it can be eaten with bread, biscuits or oatcakes; it is very good mixed with a little garlic and fresh herbs; or it can be shaped into a ball and rolled in finely chopped parsley or coarsely ground black pepper. *Makes 225 g/8 oz*

Just Desserts

*Once you have begun to try out these desserts, you
will wonder why you ever needed eggs or cream.
Use fresh fruit in season, or the simplest of
ingredients, to make the perfect dessert every time;
peaches in brandy, apricot yogurt, pancakes with
orange and lemon sauce, lime, lemon or
blackcurrant sorbet – all full of flavour, light and
refreshing.*

Geranium Creams

An unusual and very pretty dessert for a dinner party.

Per portion, without fruit: 0 g fat   140 calories/580 kJ

225 g/8 oz cottage cheese
2 tablespoons low-fat natural yogurt

4 tablespoons caster sugar
scented geranium leaves

Place the cottage cheese, yogurt and 3 tablespoons of the caster sugar in the goblet of a liquidiser and blend until smooth. Line three individual heart-shaped moulds with cheesecloth and spoon the cheese mixture into the moulds. Cover each mould with a scented geranium leaf and leave the moulds overnight on a dish to drain.

Turn out the moulds, if you like, on to a bed of freshly picked and prettily arranged geranium leaves. Sprinkle the remaining caster sugar over the top and serve the creams with fresh fruit.

Note Tiny wild strawberries, when in season, are delicious with the geranium creams. *Serves 3*

Grapes with Kirsch and Lemon Sorbet

Per portion: 0 g fat   240 calories/1000 kJ

225 g/8 oz each green and black
  grapes
3 tablespoons caster sugar
3 tablespoons kirsch

600 ml/1 pint Lemon Sorbet (page
  108)
mint sprigs to garnish

Halve the grapes and remove all the pips. Place the green grapes in one bowl and the black grapes in another. Mix together the caster sugar and kirsch and spoon the mixture over the two bowls of grapes. Place both bowls in the refrigerator to chill.

When it is time to serve, layer black grapes, green grapes and lemon sorbet in six individual tall glasses. Garnish each dessert with a sprig of mint before serving. *Serves 6 ˙*

Lemon Sorbet

(Illustrated on page 69)

Per portion: 0 g fat   180 calories/750 kJ

3 lemons   1 egg white, stiffly whisked
175 g/6 oz caster sugar

Pare the rinds of the lemons with a potato peeler and squeeze the juice.
Bring the sugar and 600 ml/1 pint of water gently to the boil, stirring until
the sugar has completely dissolved. Now boil fast for 4 minutes. Add the
lemon rinds, bring back to the boil and boil fast for a further 2 minutes. Put
the pan in a bowl of cold water to cool the syrup. Add the lemon juice. Strain
into a freezer-proof polythene carton and freeze to the mushy stage. Stir
thoroughly, turning sides to centre. Fold in the stiffly whisked egg white and
return to the freezer until firm. Keep covered in the freezer to retain the fresh
flavour.

Sorbets make the perfect end to a rich meal and really serve to liven up
jaded palates. *Serves 4*

Fresh Lime Sorbet

This is a beautiful colour and unbelievably fresh and welcome.

Per portion: 0 g fat   180 calories/750 kJ

3 limes   1 egg white, stiffly whisked
175 g/6 oz caster sugar

Pare the rinds of the limes with a potato peeler and squeeze the juice.
Dissolve the sugar in 600 ml/1 pint of water and bring to the boil. Boil for 3
minutes. Add the lime rinds and boil for a further 3 minutes, uncovered and
fast. Cool, then add the lime juice. Strain into a freezer-proof polythene
carton and freeze to the mushy stage. Stir thoroughly, turning sides to
centre, then carefully fold in the stiffly whisked egg white. Refreeze, covered,
until firm.

Serve with Tuiles d'Amandes (page 121) *Serves 4*

Blackcurrant Water Ice

(Illustrated on page 69)

Per portion: 0 g fat   270 calories/1130 kJ

225 g/8 oz sugar
450 g/1 lb blackcurrants, cooked in
   150 ml/¼ pint water

juice of 1 lemon
2 egg whites, stiffly whisked

Boil 450 ml/¾ pint of water and the sugar together for 6 minutes, to make a syrup. Cool. Blend the blackcurrants and their cooking water in a liquidiser, then press through a sieve.

Mix the cooled sugar syrup with the blackcurrant purée and lemon juice. Pour into a freezer-proof polythene carton and freeze to the mushy stage. Remove and stir thoroughly, turning sides to centre. Fold in the stiffly whisked egg whites and freeze again, carefully covered. Scoop into a chilled glass bowl to serve. *Serves 4*

Pineapple with Black Grapes

(Illustrated on page 52)

Per portion: 1 g fat   280 calories/1170 kJ

1 pineapple
275 g/10 oz black grapes
100 g/4 oz caster sugar

3 tablespoons kirsch
300 ml/½ pint low-fat natural yogurt

Peel the pineapple, cut it in half and remove the central woody core. Cut the pineapple flesh into cubes. Halve the grapes and remove all the pips.

Mix together the pineapple cubes, grapes, caster sugar, kirsch and yogurt. Place the mixture in an attractive glass bowl and chill in the refrigerator until serving time. *Serves 4*

Flamri de Semoule

The flavour of the white wine is unusual in this pretty sweet, and the fresh redcurrant sauce is truly delicious. A dinner party or family dish.

Per portion: 1 g fat   190 calories/800 kJ

225 g/8 oz redcurrants
about 2 tablespoons caster sugar to
  sweeten
150 ml/¼ pint white wine

3 tablespoons semolina
40 g/1½ oz caster sugar
2 egg whites, stiffly whisked

Purée the redcurrants in the liquidiser then sieve them to remove the tops and tails. Add about 2 tablespoons caster sugar to sweeten.

Place 300 ml/½ pint of water with the wine in a saucepan and bring to the boil. Pour in the semolina and simmer gently, stirring frequently, for about 10 minutes. Remove from the heat and cool. Beat in the remaining sugar and fold in the egg whites. Pour into a lightly oiled jelly or charlotte mould. Cover and leave in the refrigerator for several hours.

Dip the base of the mould into very hot water, then turn out the flamri on to a serving plate. Pour over the redcurrant sauce and serve with more sauce, and a bowl of yogurt, if liked.

Note Other soft fruits, such as raspberries, blackcurrants and strawberries, can also be used for the sauce. *Serves 4*

Compote of Rhubarb

(Illustrated on page 51)

Per portion: 0 g fat   100 calories/420 kJ

1 kg/2 lb rhubarb
100 g/4 oz sugar, or to taste
1 sugar cube
1 orange

1 piece preserved ginger, chopped
curls of orange rind to decorate
(optional)

Wash the rhubarb and cut it into 5-cm/2-in lengths. Barely cook the rhubarb over very low heat, with sugar to taste.

Rub the sugar cube over the orange, to become impregnated with the zest. Crush the sugar cube and add it to the rhubarb, with the chopped ginger. Chill.

This looks pretty served in a white china dish with curls of orange rind (use your potato peeler) to decorate. Hand a bowl of Home-made Yogurt separately (page 103), and a dish of dark brown sugar. *Serves 6*

Gooseberry Fool

(Illustrated on page 87)

Per portion: 1 g fat   160 calories/670 kJ

450 g/1 lb gooseberries
75 g/3 oz sugar

450 ml/$\frac{3}{4}$ pint low-fat natural yogurt
chopped nuts to decorate (optional)

Rinse the gooseberries and drain well. Cook gently with the sugar in a covered pan until the sugar has dissolved and the fruit is soft; add a little water if the fruit looks like sticking to the pan. Push the pulp through a fine sieve. Cool, then fold in the yogurt. Decorate with a few chopped nuts if you like. Serve with Brandy Snaps (page 123) and a bowl of dark brown sugar. *Serves 4*

Apricot Yogurt

Per portion: 0 g fat   210 calories/880 kJ

225 g/8 oz dried apricots
150 g/5 oz caster sugar

600 ml/1 pint low-fat natural yogurt

Soak the apricots overnight in water to cover, then cook gently for about 30 minutes, until tender. Blend in the liquidiser with a little of the cooking liquid, or press through a sieve. Add the sugar and stir well to dissolve. Cool and mix into the yogurt. Serve in individual china pots. *Serves 6*

Apricots in Wine

Total recipe: 0 g fat   1100 calories/4600 kJ

450 g/1 lb best quality dried apricots

about 300 ml/½ pint sweet white wine

Wash the apricots and pat dry with absorbent kitchen paper. Pack loosely into jars and pour on enough wine to cover. Screw on the lids tightly and leave for a week before eating.

Serve at the end of a meal with coffee.

Apricot Soufflé

Per portion: 1 g fat   230 calories/960 kJ

100 g/4 oz caster sugar
225 g/8 oz dried apricots, soaked

twist of lemon rind
4 egg whites

Lightly oil a 1-litre/2-pint soufflé dish and dust with a little of the caster sugar. Cook the apricots in their soaking water, with the lemon rind, for 30 minutes, until tender. Drain and remove the rind. Purée the apricots in a liquidiser or press them through a sieve. Stir in the remaining sugar to taste.

Whisk the egg whites until firm and fold gently and quickly into the apricot purée. Pour into the soufflé dish and cook in a moderately hot oven (200 C, 400 F, gas 6) for about 18 minutes. The soufflé should be firm sponge round the edge and creamy in the centre. *Serves 4*

Peaches in Brandy

Per portion: 0 g fat   225 calories/940 kJ

175 g/6 oz caster sugar
12 peaches

juice of 1½ lemons
4 tablespoons brandy

Dissolve the sugar in 600 ml/1 pint of water, stirring until it reaches boiling point. Boil for 6 minutes and then cool.

Pour boiling water over the peaches. Leave for 1 minute then plunge into cold water. Peel carefully, halve and remove the stones. Arrange in a beautiful glass bowl and sprinkle with the lemon juice. Add the brandy to the cooled sugar syrup and pour over the peaches. Cover with cling film and chill until required.

Serve with a pile of Baby Meringues (page 122). *Serves 6*

Pancakes St. Clements

(Illustrated on page 34)

Per portion: 2 g fat   300 calories/1250 kJ

8 cooked pancakes (page 102)
FOR THE SAUCE
1 orange, shredded, pips discarded
½ lemon, shredded, pips discarded

75 g/3 oz caster sugar
2 teaspoons cornflour
2 tablespoons orange-flavoured
   liqueur

Keep the pancakes hot while you make the sauce.

Simmer the orange, lemon, sugar and 1 tablespoon water in a covered pan for about 30 minutes, stirring occasionally. Do not allow the fruit to stick; add a little more water if necessary. Just before serving, moisten the cornflour with a little cold water and stir in enough of this mixture to thicken the sauce slightly. Finally, add the liqueur and heat through. Serve the sauce in a jug or sauceboat to pour over the hot pancakes. *Serves 4*

Celestial Bananas

A creole dish

Per portion: 1 g fat   200 calories/840 kJ

6 bananas, halved lengthways
100 g/4 oz dark soft brown sugar
juice of 1 lemon

grated rind of 1 orange
6 tablespoons rum

Lightly oil a shallow ovenproof dish and lay the bananas in the bottom. Pour over a sauce made by mixing together the remaining ingredients. Cover loosely with foil and bake in the centre of a moderately hot oven (200 C, 400 F, gas 6) for 25 minutes. Baste once or twice during cooking. *Serves 6*

Oranges with Liqueur and Praline

Per portion: 7 g fat   270 calories/1130 kJ

8 large oranges
150 ml/¼ pint orange-flavoured
  liqueur

150 g/5 oz sugar
175 g/6 oz hazelnuts, chopped

Peel the oranges entirely free of pith with a sharp knife. Divide them into segments, removing membranes and pips, and arrange in a glass serving dish. Sprinkle over the liqueur.

Dissolve the sugar very slowly in a frying pan and leave until it is a brown syrup. (Don't stir, just keep your nerve.) Add the chopped hazelnuts and stir for two minutes. Pour into a well-oiled roasting tin and leave to set. When set hard, remove the praline from the tin, wrap in a clean cloth and break up with a hammer. Sprinkle over the marinated oranges. *Serves 8*

Fresh Orange Jelly

Per portion:　0 g fat　200 calories/840 kJ

4 sugar cubes
4 oranges
75 g/3 oz caster sugar

20 g/$\frac{3}{4}$ oz powdered gelatine
juice of 1 lemon
2 oranges, segmented

Rub each sugar cube over an orange until it has absorbed as much flavour as possible. Crush the sugar cubes. Squeeze the juice from the oranges.

Put the crushed sugar, caster sugar, 300 ml/$\frac{1}{2}$ pint of water and the gelatine in a saucepan and stir over gentle heat until dissolved. Cool slightly and add the strained juice of the oranges and lemon. Pour half this jelly mixture into individual glass dishes and chill in the refrigerator until set. Keep the remaining jelly in a warmer place. When the jelly has set in the dishes, top with the fresh orange segments and pour over the rest of the jelly. Replace in the refrigerator.

This makes a refreshingly different sweet and one especially popular with children. *Serves 4*

Honey Apples

Per portion:　0 g fat　160 calories/670 kJ

4 medium-sized cooking apples,
　cored
1 tablespoon chopped nuts, toasted
1 tablespoon chopped dates

juice of $\frac{1}{2}$ lemon
about 2 tablespoons clear honey
$\frac{1}{2}$ teaspoon ground cinnamon

Wash the apples and peel the top half. Place in an ovenproof dish. Mix the remaining ingredients together and use to fill the centres of the apples. Pour a little more honey over the apples and cook, covered, in a moderately hot oven (190 C, 375 F, gas 5) for about 45 minutes. *Serves 4*

Danish Apple Charlotte

(Illustrated on page 70)

Per portion: 9 g fat   320 calories/1340kJ

50 g/2 oz fresh white breadcrumbs
75 g/3 oz sugar
1 tablespoon vegetable oil
25 g/1 oz butter or margarine

$\frac{1}{4}$ teaspoon ground cinnamon
675 g/1$\frac{1}{2}$ lb cooking apples, peeled,
   cored and sliced
100 g/4 oz raspberry jam, warmed

Mix the breadcrumbs with one-third of the sugar and fry until golden in the oil and butter or margarine. Sprinkle with the cinnamon.

Cook the apples gently with the remaining sugar in a lidded saucepan until soft. Stir occasionally to prevent sticking. Beat to a purée.

Fill a glass dish with alternate layers of crumbs, apple purée and raspberry jam, beginning and ending with a layer of crumbs. Cool and serve with a bowl of Home-made Yogurt (page 103). *Serves 4*

Cakes and Biscuits

What better on a cold winter's day than tea and cinnamon toast by the fire, with home-made fruit cake to follow? For more summery occasions, try some of these home-baked biscuits to accompany fruit desserts, fools and sorbets. And the angel cake is a deliciously light whisked sponge which can be filled with strawberries to make a real summer treat.

Fruit Cake

(Illustrated on page 88)

Perhaps not the lowest-fat cake you can make, but fine for special occasions.

Total recipe: 145 g fat   4750 calories/19900 kJ

175 g/6 oz butter or margarine
225 g/8 oz dark soft brown sugar
450 g/1 lb plain flour
½ teaspoon ground cinnamon
350 g/12 oz mixed dried fruit

3 tablespoons vinegar
175 ml/6 fl oz skimmed milk, at
room temperature
1 heaped teaspoon bicarbonate of
soda

Line an 18-cm/7-in square cake tin with oiled and floured greaseproof paper.

Cream together the butter or margarine and sugar until light. Sift the flour and cinnamon over the dried fruit in a bowl. Mix the creamed butter or margarine and sugar with the flour and fruit. Work together thoroughly.

Put the vinegar in a large bowl and add the milk. Stir in the bicarbonate of soda, watching carefully because it will froth up. Stir at once into the fruit mixture and turn into the prepared tin. Bake in a moderately hot oven (190 C, 375 F, gas 5) for 30 minutes. Lay a piece of greaseproof paper over the top of the cake, reduce the oven temperature to moderate (160 C, 325 F, gas 3) and bake for a further 1½ hours.

Tuiles d'Amandes

Very good, delicate and crisp. A lovely accompaniment to fruit desserts such as fools and sorbets.

Per biscuit: 3 g fat   70 calories/290 kJ

2 egg whites
90 g/3½ oz caster sugar, sifted
50 g/2 oz plain flour, sifted
¼ teaspoon vanilla essence

¼ teaspoon almond essence
25 g/1 oz almonds, shredded
50 g/2 oz butter or margarine,
    melted but not hot

Whisk together the egg whites and caster sugar until thick. Fold in the sifted flour. Add the vanilla and almond essences, shredded almonds and butter or margarine and mix all carefully together.

Line two large baking trays with non-stick baking paper and put small spoonfuls of the mixture on each, spaced well apart (the biscuits will spread out while cooking).

Bake in a moderately hot oven (190 C, 375 F, gas 5) for about 6 minutes, until pale gold. Remove from the oven, lift off the tuiles while still warm and curl quickly round a rolling pin. Cool on a wire tray and store carefully in an airtight tin. *Makes about 18*

Baby Meringues

Per meringue: 0 g fat   30 calories/130 kJ

3 egg whites   175 g/6 oz caster sugar

Whisk the egg whites until they are stiff. Add 2 tablespoons of the caster sugar and whisk again until the mixture is really stiff and glossy. Gently fold in the remaining caster sugar with a metal spoon; do not over-stir or you will knock the air out of the meringue mixture.

Line a large baking tray with non-stick baking paper. Using a piping bag fitted with a star nozzle, pipe the meringue on to the paper in small star shapes. Bake in a very cool oven (110 C, 225 F, gas $\frac{1}{4}$) for about 4 hours, until the meringues can be easily removed from the paper with a palette knife. Place the meringues in a warm place to dry out thoroughly. *Makes about 24*

Brandy Snaps

(Illustrated on page 88)

Per brandy snap: 6 g fat   70 calories/280 kJ

100 g/4 oz golden syrup
100 g/4 oz dark soft brown sugar
100 g/4 oz butter or margarine
2 teaspoons lemon juice

100 g/4 oz plain flour
$\frac{1}{4}$ teaspoon salt
1 teaspoon ground ginger

Place the golden syrup, brown sugar and butter or margarine in a heavy-bottomed saucepan. Heat gently, stirring constantly, until the sugar has melted. Cool slightly and then stir in the lemon juice. Sift together the flour, salt and ground ginger and fold the dry ingredients into the syrup mixture.

Line several baking sheets with non-stick baking paper. Place small spoonfuls of the brandy snap mixture, spaced well apart, on to the baking sheets. Cook for 8 minutes in a moderate oven (160 C, 325 F, gas 3). Allow to cool for a minute, then lift with a palette knife and shape the brandy snaps round the handle of a wooden spoon whilst they are still warm. Cool completely on a wire tray and store in an airtight tin. *Makes about 30*

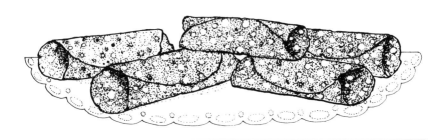

Angel Cake

(Illustrated on page 88)

This can be filled with strawberries which have been sprinkled with caster sugar and a little lemon juice, or it can be iced with a glacé icing – either white or chocolate.

Total recipe: 0 g fat   850 calories/3550 kJ

40 g/1½ oz plain flour	5 egg whites
25 g/1 oz cornflour	¼ teaspoon salt
1 teaspoon baking powder	½ teaspoon cream of tartar
125 g/4½ oz caster sugar	1 teaspoon vanilla essence

Sift the first three ingredients together several times to incorporate air and to blend them well. Sift the caster sugar with a tablespoon of the flour mixture.

Whisk the egg whites with the salt and cream of tartar until quite stiff. Fold in the dry ingredients very quickly and gently, then sprinkle on and fold in the vanilla essence.

Pour into a lightly oiled and floured ring tin. Cook in a moderately hot oven (190 C, 375 F, gas 5) for about 25 minutes, until the cake feels springy and shrinks slightly from the sides of the tin. Invert on to a wire rack to cool, and turn out of the tin when cold.

Cinnamon Toast

Really good news, as P. G. Wodehouse would have said, for a winter's afternoon.

Per portion: **6 g fat**   **190 calories/790 kJ**

6 slices white bread
40 g/1½ oz butter or margarine to
  spread

3 tablespoons dark soft brown sugar
2 teaspoons ground cinnamon

Toast the bread on both sides and spread with butter or margarine on one side while still hot. Mix together the sugar and cinnamon and sprinkle on to the hot toast. Place under the grill until the sugar bubbles. Cut into fingers and serve immediately. *Serves 6*

Index

Fish pie 47
Garlic and tarragon sauce for steamed fish 48
Flamri de semoule 111
French beans and mushrooms vinaigrette 89
French onion soup 32
Fruit cake 120

Garlic sauce 100
Garlic and tarragon sauce for steamed fish 48
Gazpacho 36
Geranium creams 106
Gooseberry fool 112
Grape:
  Grapes with kirsch and lemon sorbet 107
  Pineapple with black grapes 110
Grapefruit-watercress cocktail 18
Gravad lax 22

Haddock:
  Fish pie 47
  Kedgeree 43
Hallowe'en chicken with sauce diable 73
Ham in parsley jelly 53
Hare:
  Civet de lièvre 81
Honey apples 117
Horseradish sauce 63

Iced cucumber soup 29
Italian leek and pumpkin soup 26
Italian veal casserole 59

Kedgeree 43

Lamb:
  Lamb korma 56
  Moussaka 57
  Navarin de mouton 55
  Roast lamb 54
Leek:
  Italian leek and pumpkin soup 26
  Vichyssoise 31
Lemon:
  Cold lemon chicken 76
  Lemon sorbet 108
Lime:
  Fresh lime sorbet 108

Mackerel with lemon and bay leaves 39
Mackerel with yogurt and chives 39
Melon with vermouth 21

Meringues 122
Moussaka 57
Mushroom:
  French beans and mushrooms vinaigrette 89
  Mushroom sauce 101
  Mushrooms en cocotte 18
  Spaghetti with mushrooms 91
Mustard sauce 99

Navarin de mouton 55

Obbie's salad 93
Old English casserole of beef 62
Onion:
  French onion soup 32
Orange:
  Fresh orange jelly 117
  Oranges with liqueur and praline 116

Pancake batter 102
Pancakes St. Clements 115
Paprika chicken 72
Peach and ginger salad 92
Peaches in brandy 114
Pepper:
  Stuffed green peppers 23
Pheasant:
  Faisan en casserole 80
Pineapple:
  Pineapple with black grapes 110
  Port of Spain prawns 24
  Rice pilaf 86
Plaice with mushrooms and cider 41
Polly's lapin à la moutarde 82
Pork:
  Porc à l'orange 54
  Porc aux pruneaux 50
Port of Spain prawns 24
Portuguese cod 42
Potato:
  Riced potatoes 86
Prawn:
  Port of Spain prawns 24
Psari plaki 40
Pumpkin:
  Italian leek and pumpkin soup 26

Rabbit:
  Polly's lapin à la moutarde 82
Ratatouille 94
Red cabbage 84
Rhubarb compote 112
Rice pilaf 86
Rice salad 92
Riced potatoes 86

127

Salads 77, 91–3
Salmon:
 Cold salmon 45
 Gravad lax 22
 Salmon mousse 44
 Salmon parcels 46
Saltimbocca 58
Sauce diable 73
Sauces 96–101
Smoked fish starters 20
Soft curd cheese 104
Sorbets 108
Soup:
 Carrot and tomato soup 30
 Country vegetable soup 27
 Courgette and cucumber soup 28
 French onion soup 32
 Iced cucumber soup 29
 Italian leek and pumpkin soup 26
 Spinach soup 28
 Vichyssoise 31
 Walnut soup 26
 Winter vegetable soup 32
Soured cream, low-fat 101
Spaghetti alla marinara 61
Spaghetti with mushrooms 91
Spinach:
 Eggs florentine 23
 Spinach soup 28
Starters:
 Eggs florentine 23
 Fresh tomato juice cocktail 20
 Grapefruit-watercress cocktail 18
 Gravad lax 22
 Les crudités 24
 Melon with vermouth 21
 Mushrooms en cocotte 18
 Port of Spain prawns 24
 Smoked fish 20
 Stuffed green peppers 23

Tagliatelle romana 21
Tomates farcies duxelles 19
Stuffed green peppers 23
Stuffed pot-roasted chicken 68
Swedish meatballs 60

Tagliatelle romana 21
Tomato:
 Carrot and tomato soup 30
 Fresh tomato juice cocktail 20
 Fresh tomato soup 35
 Gazpacho 36
 Tomates farcies duxelles 19
 Tomato sauce 97
Topinambours provençale 90
Trout with almonds 40
Tuiles d'amandes 121
Turkey:
 Traditional roast turkey 78
 Turkey in vermouth 79

Veal:
 Italian veal casserole 59
 Saltimbocca 58
Vegetable. *See also* Artichoke, Carrot etc.
 Country vegetable soup 27
 Les crudités 24
 Ratatouille 94
 Winter vegetable soup 32
Velouté sauce 97
Vichyssoise 31

Walnut soup 26
Winter vegetable soup 32

Yogurt:
 Apricot yogurt 113
 Home-made yogurt 103
 Mackerel with yogurt and chives 39
 Yogurt dressing 103